USE SCRAPS, SEW BLOCKS, MAKE
100 QUILTS

PAVILION

CONTENTS

INTRODUCTION

I've been making and designing quilts for over 25 years and without question my favourite type are scrap quilts. Whether made from the remnants of other assorted projects or from my ever-expanding fabric collection, I love their vibrancy, their eclecticism, their joy and their spontaneity.

Fabric is the driving force behind our creative pursuits, but sometimes it threatens to overwhelm us and take over our homes. Collecting fabric and keeping our scraps is a wonderful thing, but at some point it's important to allow those fabrics to fulfil their destiny and be part of something magical.

I hope you will find inspiration in this collection of 100 scrap blocks and quilts. Whether you are a modern or traditional quilter, prefer appliqué or paper piecing, whether your heart is in the country or you're a dedicated city dweller, there is, I hope, much here to tempt and excite you.

Before you get cracking, do give the first few chapters the once over. You'll find tips, techniques and tuition to make sure your quiltmaking is satisfying and successful. Even if you're a seasoned sewer, it's great to refresh your knowledge and find out about some of the innovations which can help us make our quilts faster, easier and more accurately. If you've never made a quilt before but always dreamed of doing so it's even more important to read the technique and equipment chapters thoroughly before you start. There's no need to feel intimidated by any of the patterns but if you are brand new to sewing or quilting go for a design with larger, simpler shapes like squares and rectangles and keep your first few projects small and manageable. Whatever your skill level, I always recommend you make a test block before you commit to making the whole quilt.

Each of the 100 patterns can be used to make a quilt and you'll find suggestions for settings, sashings, borders and colour schemes with every pattern. Use these patterns as they are or adapt them to make a quilt that is uniquely you. Mix and match the border treatments, colours and arrangements as you see fit. Change the size of the quilts by adding more blocks and rows or by increasing the size of each block. Add extra borders or wider sashings to make the quilt fit the space you have.

Make the quilts your own... Celebrate your fabric collection and liberate your scraps!

WHAT IS A SCRAP QUILT?

Oh my, I think we just opened a can of worms! Let's talk about the strict definitions first and take it from there. For some, a scrap quilt is one that features a huge variety of different fabrics and in which pretty much every block uses something unique and no two are quite the same. For others, a scrap quilt must use oddments, remnants and leftovers from previous quilting and dressmaking endeavours. A scrap quilt might also be one in which every fabric was purchased specifically for that quilt and no other. In the context of a juried quilt show, a scrap quilt may have to contain a specific minimum number of different fabrics to qualify.

All of these definitions make sense to me and I have made each type of scrap quilt in my time. Most of the quilts I make would fit the definition of a scrap quilt to some extent. For me a scrap quilt is more of an attitude, an idea, or a look, rather than a rigid definition made up by someone else... in a word, it's PERSONAL! There are certain factors that really matter to me when I'm planning or making a scrap quilt.

I want variety

I want as many different fabrics in my quilt as I can possibly get. I'm a fabric addict, but I'm not a hoarder – I buy fabrics to use them. Scrap quilts allow me to use a lot of different fabrics in one glorious quilt. Variety also allows me to introduce new fabrics even when I'm three quarters of the way through making a top and I run out of a fabric. There's no panic, no drama, no 2am trawl through the internet trying to find a piece of fabric printed ten years ago. I simply pop in a new fabric that works with the others. Doesn't that sound like a civilized way of doing things?

I want my colour choices to work

I am not an artist in the strictest sense. I have an innate sense of whether something is 'right' or 'wrong' and I believe that is in all of us. We all struggle to get the 'right' mix sometimes, so I use variety to make my choices work. If I use just one red fabric in a quilt and it's the wrong red, well then it might make the whole quilt 'wrong'. If I use that red plus twenty others, the individual fabric won't matter as much. It becomes 'right'. Yay! In a nutshell, why use one red when I can use twenty, or thirty or a hundred?

I want visual interest

I want to feel drawn into my quilt, so that the more I look, the more I see. I want other people to see the whole quilt and to love it but to then take a closer look and see the individual elements. If I can surprise the viewer with some of my choices, so much the better, so I need variety of tone, texture, colour and pattern – the more the better!

I want my quilt to keep on giving

If my quilt is made of one block, repeated twenty times, and I use the same fabrics in every block, why do I need to make the whole quilt? I could just save time and make one block, because the whole quilt won't give me any more for the extra time spent. If every block is different, with a wide variety of fabrics, but I use a design that creates a cohesive whole, then I will get a quilt that works as an entity in its own right – but there is also plenty to draw me in further.

I want to dent my stash

My quilts often contain fabrics that I already had, waiting patiently in a pile, a box, a drawer or the back of a cupboard. Some of my fabrics get used when they are shiny and new, others wait a while before they get their moment. I use yardage, pre-cuts, offcuts and leftovers, whatever I have that works in my design. I rarely go out and buy everything to make a quilt in one shopping trip. The benefit of using fabrics that you already have are twofold. First, you can get started right away whilst you are full of inspiration and motivation to create. Second, there's no cost or outlay required to make a start on your scrap quilt. A well-stocked stash is like having money in the bank!

Your colour choices can make or break your scrap quilt, so think carefully about your fabrics before you start and don't be afraid to make a test block or a 'paste-up' before you begin!.

MAKING COLOURS WORK

Without going into a whole lesson on the colour wheel, here are a few simple tips that can make your colour choices work, particularly when you make a scrap quilt.

Throw everything at it

The whole kit and caboodle, the full nine yards, the kitchen sink, too, if you like! This is particularly successful when the fabrics are sorted into lights and darks (and possibly mediums) and the value (the lightness or darkness) is consistent throughout the quilt.

Use one colour plus a neutral

One of my favourite colour combinations is blue (or red) with cream, but in the best scrap traditions make sure that the blues (or reds) go from light to dark and every shade and permutation in between and that the creams range from white to tan.

Throw in another colour

Here's where a little knowledge of the colour wheel helps. Choose complementary colours – for example, blue and orange – but use every shade of blue and orange you can find. For real sparkle and punch, add in some blues that are greenish or purplish and some oranges that have reds and pinks mixed in.

'Neutral' goes way beyond white and cream

Black, navy and red are all amazing 'neutrals', but so are chocolate or rust – and don't get me started on mustard yellow!

Pay it forward

Having a well-stocked stash is not only fun to acquire, it also makes the creative process so much easier and potentially more successful.

Don't feel bad if you have to go fabric shopping to make a scrap quilt work (as if!)

You may need to add some fat quarters, a layer cake, a couple of half yards or even four or five yards of background fabric to make the scraps that you have work well. Remember, 'scrap quilting' is an attitude, not a prison sentence. Make it work in whatever way suits you.

ORGANIZING YOUR SCRAPS

Keeping your scraps in an organized and 'ready to use' state is so much more appealing than wading through a massive pile of creased and tangled bits heaped up on the floor of your sewing room! Follow my scrap storage tips and you'll always be ready to sew!

1 Organize your scraps into piles of the same or a similar colour. Depending on the quantity you have or the type of quilt you intend to make, you might further sort the fabrics into lights, mediums and darks or sort them by genre – for example, novelty, Christmas or Asian-themed.

2 Give each fabric a good iron to remove the wrinkles. Assess what you have.

3 Remove any tangled threads or tiny off-cuts that will be of no use to you. Be brutal here: there's no point storing little bits you will never realistically use. Your trash may be someone else's treasure, so consider gifting these bits to a friend or your local quilt guild.

Your preparation may well end here... Fold your fabric neatly and stack on shelves or in drawers ready for use. However, I recommend going a few steps further!

4 Trim off any odd-shaped chunks, leaving as large a remaining piece as possible. Store this larger piece with others of a similar colour or value. Use acid-free mount board or plastic boards designed for comic book collectors. Wrapped around these boards your 'mini-bolts' will look appealing, making them so much more likely to be used!

5 Trim any oddments down to a size and shape you commonly use, for example 2½" (6.4cm) squares or a 1½" (3.8cm) strip.

6 Keep a box/wallet or drawer specifically for your home-made 'pre-cuts' and some day in the not-too-distant future, you will have the pieces already cut for a project.

7 If you love making strip quilts cut a 2½" (6.4cm) strip off every fabric that you have and keep them together in a drawer or box. You can do the same with charm squares (5"/12.7cm squares) or layer cakes (10"/25.4cm squares). Before you know it, you will have the equivalent of a commercial pre-cut pack without the additional financial outlay!

8 Consider purchasing a storage unit for your scraps. I have several, which house plastic bins and drawers labelled by colour plus one for 'odds and ends'.

9 When your scraps are organized, it's much clearer to see what you have and what you don't. You may be overrun with 'mediums' but lacking in lights and darks, which can make planning a quilt challenging. Consider a fabric exchange with other quilters to even out your scraps (and theirs!).

10 If you're storing folded fabrics on open shelving, make sure they are protected from strong sunlight. Fabric can fade really quickly if it's exposed to a south-facing window. Install a roller blind at the top of your shelving unit that can be pulled down to protect your precious stash.

TECHNIQUES, TOOLS AND MATERIALS

ROTARY CUTTING

For the majority of my quiltmaking I use the rotary cutting system. When you know how, it's very accurate, fast and easy to do. You'll need what I like to call the 'Holy Trinity': three very important pieces of equipment.

Rotary cutter Essentially a circular blade mounted on a handle, as you push away the blade rotates and cuts through up to eight layers of fabric. Beginners should start with cutting one layer at a time and build up to more. My own cut-off is four layers; beyond that I find I get ruler slippage. The most useful size cutter to buy is one with a 1¾" (44mm) blade, although larger and smaller ones are available.

Rotary cutting ruler An ⅛" (3mm) thick perspex ruler made specifically to use with a rotary cutter, it is marked with a grid of inches or centimetres, plus smaller increments. The fabric is measured and cut using the ruler, so marking on shapes is not necessary. Most also have lines showing the 45 and 60 degree angles. The most useful size to buy is 24" x 6" (61 x 15.2cm), although other sizes are available. Do not substitute any other kind of ruler – you must use one designed specifically for rotary cutters!

Self-healing mat This goes on your work surface – the fabric and ruler go on top and then you cut. The mat protects your table from the blade and also has grid lines printed on it to help you measure and square up fabric. The most useful size to buy is 18" x 24" (45.7 x 61cm) – slightly bigger than an A2 piece of paper. Keep your mat flat at all times. Don't prop it up against a wall overnight, as it will warp and will never go flat again.

First things first!

Get the iron out and press those fabrics. Even fabric that has come straight off the bolt needs pressing. Those scraps that have been lingering in a pile will definitely need straightening out! Press well, and use steam. I like to use a spray of ordinary laundry starch, too – it makes the fabric a little crisper for cutting and it will be easier to piece.

Straightening the edge of fabric

Start by straightening the edge on your fabric. Fold the fabric, selvedge to selvedge, and place it on your mat with the fold at the top. Align a straight line on your ruler with the fold and hold the ruler firmly down with your left hand. Stick out your little finger and place it on the fabric to help steady your hand. Push the blade of your rotary cutter out, position it against the ruler about 1" (2.5cm) below the start of your fabric on the right-hand side (if you are right handed – reverse the process for left handers) and push the blade firmly up the edge of the ruler. Once you have cut about 6" (15.2cm) of fabric, you will need to stop cutting and move your left hand up the ruler before continuing to cut to prevent the ruler from slipping.

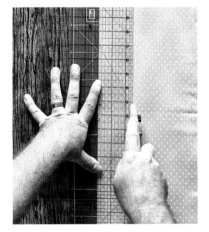

Cutting strips

Turn the mat so that the straightened edge is on the left and the fold is at the bottom. Do this in preference to turning the fabric: you've just cut a perfectly straight edge and turning the fabric will disturb that edge! Position your ruler on top of the fabric, with the bottom of the ruler lined up with the fold and the width of strip you require under the ruler. Use the grid lines on the ruler to measure the strip width. The fabric to the right of the ruler is not covered and is spare. Position the cutter at the bottom of the ruler, blade out, and push it out along the ruler edge. If you require more strips, simply move the ruler over to the right the required width and cut again. If the strip you require is wider than your ruler, just turn your ruler on its side. You now have 24" (61cm) of ruler to work with instead of 6" (15.2cm). Cut about 6", then move the ruler along and continue to cut.

Cutting rectangles, squares and triangles

Cut strips to the required width, then sub-cut those strips into rectangles or squares. Cut rectangles or squares on the diagonal to make triangles.

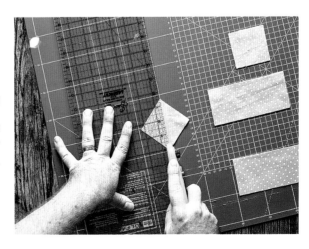

Cutting patches from irregular scraps

You can cut squares, rectangles and all kinds of other patches from your irregular little scraps, too. First determine the 'straight of grain'. That's easy on a full width of fabric, as it runs parallel to the selvedge, but on a small scrap you'll need to look closer. You want the weave of the fabric to be as straight as possible when you make that first cut. Straighten one edge, keeping the straight edge 'on grain', and then use that cut edge to line up your ruler for the second, third and subsequent cuts.

USING TEMPLATES

Some shapes can't be cut using a rotary cutter. The Drunkard's Path block (page 120) is a good example. I've seen people freehand cutting curves with a rotary cutter, but for safety reasons I don't recommend it! It is much better to make a template and cut shapes out with scissors. You can cut templates for many simple straight-edged shapes, too. This is particularly useful if you only have scissors.

My favourite template material is a wonderful thing called 'freezer paper'. You can get it from quilt shops and online. It's an American product and is used to wrap meat for the freezer. I would love to meet the quilter who discovered its many uses for patchwork – it really is wonderful. Freezer paper has a matte paper side and a shiny waxy side. To use it, trace the desired shape carefully onto the matte paper side. Use a ruler for straight edges and make sure that the template you are tracing has the ¼" (6mm) seam allowance added (all of the templates in this book do!). Cut the paper template out carefully with scissors.

If you only have a few shapes to cut, then simply iron the freezer paper onto the fabric, shiny side down, then cut out the shape. The paper will peel off when you're all cut out and can be re-used a number of times. If you need to cut hundreds of a shape, then it's worth ironing your freezer paper to thin card to make a more durable template. You can also buy template plastic, but keep your iron away from it... it melts!

DIE CUTTING

Fabric cutting has experienced something of an evolution over the last few decades, with most of us shunning scissors for the faster and more accurate rotary-cutting route. A few years ago I discovered fabric die cutting and it is now a favourite way for me to quickly and accurately cut and prepare my fabrics for quilting. My favourite AccuQuilt Go! cutter is pictured above.

In a nutshell, die cutting works in much the same way as a cookie cutter, stamping through multiple layers of fabric in one go to create perfect shapes every time. Each 'die' cuts a particular shape in a particular size – and because quilters use a lot of the same size and shape pieces for almost endless variations, it isn't necessary to have a huge collection of dies in order to make great quilts!

Fabric is layered on top of the chosen die in a 'fan' or 'concertina' fold. Generally, home-use dies will cut up to six layers of cotton fabric. A special self-healing mat is placed on top of the fabric and then the die/fabric/mat sandwich is sent through a die-cutting machine – essentially a set of hand- or electric-cranked rollers that press the blades through the fabric. Die cutting comes into its own when complex shapes are required or when a huge number of pieces are needed. Die cutting is also a great choice for quilters with mobility or strength issues in their hands or arms.

As a 'basic tool kit' for die cutting, I recommend the following:

- 6½" square (6" finished)
- 3½" square (3" finished)
- Half square triangle – 6" finished square
- Quarter square triangle – 6" finished square
- Half square triangle – 3" finished square
- Square on point – 4¾" (4¼" finished)
- Parallelogram 45° – 3¹¹⁄₁₆" x 4¹⁵⁄₁₆" (3" x 4¼" finished)
- Rectangle – 3½" x 6 ½" (3" x 6" finished)

Dies can be purchased individually or in sets. I also get great use out of my 1½" and 2½" strip cutting dies.

Whenever I have a bunch of scraps left over at the end of a project, I run the remainders through my die cutter and cut a variety of these 'basic shapes' and store them ready for future use.

PIECING

Patchwork is sewn with a ¼" seam and if everything is going to fit together easily and perfectly then accuracy really counts! You may have a ¼" or 'patchwork' foot for your sewing machine, which is handy but doesn't guarantee accuracy – only you can control that! Try this handy exercise to see if you're sewing an accurate ¼" seam. If you work in metric you will need to use a 6mm seam allowance for patchwork. Follow the same process as for imperial sewers but use a metric ruler. Stick to one system, imperial (inches) or metric (centimetres). Don't mix the two!

The perfect seam

Cut three pieces of fabric, each 2½" x 4½" (6.4 x 11.4cm). Using your ¼" foot sew two of the strips together along the long edge, then press the seam one way. Now add the third rectangle to the top. It should fit perfectly... but does it?

2½" + 2½" minus two ¼" seam allowances should equal 4½"

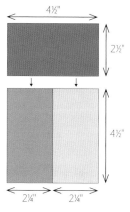

If the third strip is too long, your seam allowance is too big and needs slimming down. If it's too small, your seam allowance is a bit on the skinny side and needs fattening up. It's easy to make small adjustments now before you start on a project.

If you don't have a ¼" foot for your sewing machine but are able to move your needle position, you can use the regular foot to sew a perfect ¼" seam allowance. Generally you need to move your needle position over to the right a bit... this is usually done by adjusting the stitch width while in straight stitch mode. Place your rotary ruler under the foot of your machine, with the edge of the ruler aligned with the edge of your presser foot. Hand crank the needle down until the tip just touches the ruler. Keep moving the needle position and hand cranking the needle down to touch the ruler until it is just on the ¼" mark. Take a note of the needle position for future reference. If you can't move the needle position, place your ruler as before, so that the needle just touches the ¼" mark, then place a strip of masking tape onto the bed of your sewing machine. Use this tape as a guide for your fabric.

Check your ¼" seam allowance regularly! I like to make a unit, for example, a four patch then measure it and check that it is the correct size. Then make one block in its entirety and measure it. It's much better to know that adjustments are needed now, before you make the remaining 99 blocks!

Sewing patches

1. Place the fabrics right sides together.
2. Match the ends first and pin.
3. Sew the seam using a stitch length of approximately 2.2–2.6.
4. Clip the threads as you go.
5. Press seams one way, usually towards the darker fabric to avoid show-through.

Strip piecing

Construction can be made faster by sewing strips of fabric together and then cutting segments from this panel. This really speeds the process of patchwork up, particularly when sewing units with squares and rectangles.

1. Place two strips right sides together and pin.
2. Sew the seam using a slightly shorter than normal stitch length – a stitch length of 2 is perfect.
3. Press the seam one way, usually towards the darker fabric.
4. Continue to add strips and press until your strip-pieced panel is complete.
5. Cross-cut your panel into suitably sized segments. These can then be pieced with other strips.

String piecing

Some of the quilts in this book use 'string piecing', which is a technique whereby thin strips and scraps are pieced together to form a larger piece of fabric, that is then cut to the correct size.

1. Sew your first two strips together using a ¼" (6mm) seam allowance.
2. Press the seam one way.
3. Continue to add strips and press the seams until your panel is large enough or you have used up all the available fabric.
4. If a strip of fabric is not long enough to add to the panel, sew several together to make the required length. Join this 'pieced strip' to the panel and continue.
5. Cut your patches from this newly made 'fabric'.

BASIC PATCHWORK UNITS

There are just a few basic patchwork units that seem to crop up all the time. Here are my favourite methods to produce these quickly and accurately.

Half square triangle (HST) unit

To calculate the size of fabric you need to cut for the HST, start with the finished size. For example, 3" (7.6cm) finished: add ⅞" (2.2cm) and cut two squares to this size, ie 3⅞" (9.8cm). Proceed as follows.

1. Pair two squares right sides together and mark one diagonal with a pencil. Sew ¼" (6mm) either side of the pencil line.
2. Cut apart on the drawn line. Open up the HST units and press the seams one way.
3. Trim the seams neatly as shown.

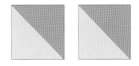

Quarter square triangle (QST) or hourglass units

To calculate the size of fabric you need to cut for the QST, start with the finished size. For example, 3" (7.6cm) finished: add 1¼" (3.2cm) and cut two squares to this size, ie 4¼" (10.8cm). Proceed as follows.

1. Pair two squares right sides together and mark both diagonals with a pencil.
2. Sew ¼" (6mm) away from the pencil line to the centre, on the same side of each quarter triangle, as shown.
3. Cut apart on the drawn lines. Open up the pieces and press the seams one way.
4. Rejoin the units in pairs to yield two units.

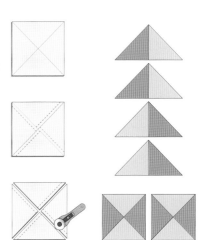

Stitch and flip

This is a great method for adding triangles to larger blocks and is sometime referred to as 'snowballing'.

1. Take one small square and lightly mark the diagonal on the wrong side with a pencil. Place this small square, right sides together, on the top of the larger square with the diagonal line running across the corner. Repeat with a second smaller square on the opposite corner.
2. Pin, then stitch on the marked diagonal. Trim the corner away, flip the corner back and press.

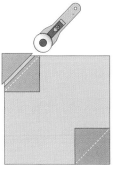

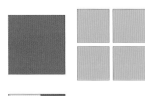

Flying geese unit (FG) – 'no-waste' method

To calculate the size of fabric you need to cut for the FG, start with the finished size.

Fabric A (goose): finished width of FG unit + 1¼" (3.2cm)
Fabric B (sky): finished width of FG unit + ⅞" (2.2cm)
Proceed as follows.

1. Cut one square of fabric A and four squares of fabric B.
2. Place two of the smaller squares on top of the larger square, right sides together, as shown.
3. Mark the diagonal, through the two small squares, with a pencil.
4. Sew ¼" (6mm) either side of the pencil line. Cut along the drawn line.
5. Working on one of the halves, flip back the two small square halves and press.
6. Add another small square, right sides together, as shown. Mark the diagonal, and sew ¼" (6mm) either side of the pencil line.
7. Cut along the drawn line, flip the small triangle over and press again.
8. Repeat with the remaining pieces half created in step 4. You will have four flying geese units.

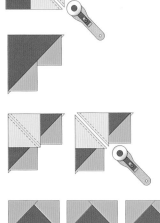

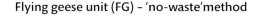

PAPER FOUNDATION PIECING

This is one of my favourite patchwork techniques and once you try it, I'm sure it will become one of yours too. Don't confuse paper piecing with English paper piecing (EPP) – that's a hand sewn technique and not the same thing at all! So what is paper foundation piecing? Essentially it involves machine-sewing fabric directly to a sheet of paper, printed with the patchwork block pattern. Fabric is placed on the non-printed side of the pattern and you sew on the printed side, following the lines. It's easy when you know how!

Let's start with an easy block, the square in a square.

1. Download and print (see page 224 for link) or photocopy one copy of Square in a Square foundation A (page 235). Make sure that you print it actual size and then measure the printed foundation. It should measure 4½" x 4½" (11.4 x 11.4cm) up to the dashed outer line.

2. Pre-cutting your fabric patches makes sewing the block much easier. I cut out shapes that are at least ½" (12mm) bigger on all sides than the finished size. Using a rotary cutter means that you can cut multiple blocks in one go.

3. Gather your supplies. You'll need some fairly fine (60wt) cotton or polyester thread in a neutral colour for piecing, an open-toed foot for your sewing machine, pins, your sewing machine and a pair of scissors. You'll also need a piece of card... a postcard is ideal!

4. Set up your sewing machine: neutral thread in the top and bobbin, a new needle (size 75 microtex is my favourite) then set your stitch length to shorter than normal – a stitch length of between 1 and 1.5 is perfect for paper piecing. Try sewing a piece of paper... the paper should perforate and come apart easily when pulled, but it shouldn't disintegrate as you're sewing.

5. Place your first piece of fabric on the back of foundation A (here, the middle square), right side facing UP. It should cover patch number 1 completely and hang over into the surrounding patches by at least ¼" (6mm). Hold the foundation up to a light source and check! Pin in place. Place patch number 2 on top of patch 1, right side DOWN, raw edges lined up. Pin in place.

6. Turn the foundation over so that the printed side is facing up and sew on the line between patches 1 and 2. Make sure that you start and finish sewing at least ¼" (6mm) over the end of the patch.

7. Flip the foundation so the fabric is facing you, and press patch number 2 back. Hold it up to the light and make sure that is has properly covered number 2 and extends into the surrounding patches by at least ¼" (6mm).

8. Add patches 3, 4 and 5 in the same manner, one at a time, sewing, flipping back and pressing each time.

If your fabric pieces are too big, you can trim the excess away. Place a postcard on top of the foundation against the next seam line and fold the paper back against it. This will reveal the overhanging fabric underneath. Place your rotary ruler on top and trim the excess away, leaving a ¼" (6mm) seam allowance. This makes lining the next patch up very easy!

 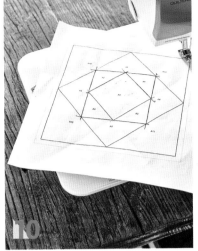 

9. Add patches 6, 7, 8 and 9 in the same way.

10. Turn the foundation over so that the paper side is facing up.

11. Use a rotary cutter, ruler and mat to trim the block along the outside lines. Be careful here! Use the outer line to trim so that the final ¼" (6mm) seam allowance is included.

12. Leave the paper intact until all sides of the block have been sewn to something else. Remove the paper by tearing along the sewn lines. The paper should come away very easily but if it doesn't you can lightly spritz with water and leave to soften for 30 seconds. A pair of tweezers is handy for removing tiny pieces of paper left in the seam intersections.

Some blocks require you to make several different foundations (labelled A, B, C etc.). If that's the case, sew the foundations separately, then trim the blocks to the outer line (this includes the ¼"/6mm seam allowance). Place foundations A and B right sides together, then sew along the final printed line. I like to use a very long basting stitch (stitch length 5 or 6) for doing this. I can then check for correct alignment. If I'm out at all, I can easily remove the basting stitches and have another go. If everything is perfect, I re-sew the seam using a very short stitch length (1–1.5).

23

APPLIQUÉ

Appliqué is the process whereby one fabric is laid on top of another and sewn down (or 'applied'), and is a perennial favourite for quilters. Appliqué can be 'raw edge' or 'turned edge' and both techniques are easy to learn.

Raw edge or fused appliqué

For this technique you will need a background fabric, fabric for the appliqués and fusible web. This is available from a variety of manufacturers and in several different weights, including a heavy weight that does not need sewing at all. Make sure you are using fusible web designed for appliqué (as opposed to fusible interfacing). You'll also need thread to match or contrast with your appliqué fabrics.

1. Trace the shape to be appliquéd onto the paper side of the fusible web. Keep in mind that your finished appliqué will be the reverse of your traced image, so letters and numbers (for example) should be reversed for tracing.
2. Roughly cut the shape out of fusible web, leaving approximately ½" (12mm) allowance around your traced image.
3. Fuse the web to the wrong side of your chosen appliqué fabric. It is a good idea to protect the sole plate of your iron from the fusible web by covering the appliqué fabric with baking parchment.
4. When the fabric has cooled, cut the appliqué shape out accurately on your drawn line.
5. Remove the paper backing and lay the appliqué shape on your chosen background fabric in its final position.
6. Iron the appliqué shape in place. Refer to the manufacturer's instructions for the correct heat setting.
7. Sew around the edge of your appliqué with matching or contrasting thread to neaten the raw edges and provide more durability. You can use a small zig zag stitch or a blanket stitch to do this.

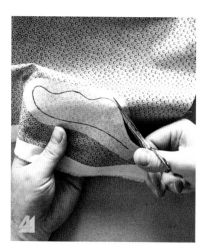 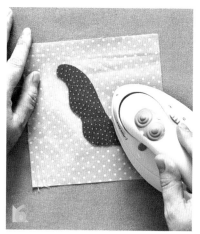 

Turned edge appliqué

Turned edge appliqué is a great choice for quilts that will be used and washed a lot, since the raw edges are turned under before stitching. Traditionally this is done by 'needle turning', but this is a slow and laborious process. I have two methods that I prefer to use to turn the edge.

'SOFT-EDGE' TURNED APPLIQUÉ

1. Trace the appliqué shape on to the smooth side of a piece of lightweight fusible interfacing (the kind used for dressmaking) and cut it out roughly.

2. Place the interfacing glue side to right side of your chosen appliqué fabric and sew around the traced shaped, on the drawn line. Use a slightly smaller stitch than normal (2.0 is spot on!).

3. Trim the seam down to a scant ¼" (6mm) and clip the curves. Make a small slip in the back of the interfacing and turn through to the right side.

4. Run the tip of your scissors or a blunt tool, such as a chopstick, around the edge of the shape and flatten with your hand.

5. Place the appliqué shape on your chosen background fabric and iron in place, then sew around the shape by hand or machine.

STARCH AND PRESS APPLIQUÉ

1. Trace the appliqué shape onto thin card... a piece of cereal box is ideal. Cut out neatly, following your drawn line.

2. Cut your chosen appliqué fabric ¼" (6mm) bigger than the card shape on all sides.

3. Paint the ¼" (6mm) of extra fabric with liquid starch. Just spray starch from a can into a small cup and wait till the bubbles settle. Dip a fine paintbrush into the liquid and 'paint' the edges of your appliqué. You want them fully wetted but not dripping!

4. Place the card template on top of the wrong side of the fabric, then use a small iron (a travel iron works for me!) to lift the wetted edge up and over onto the card. Press in place for a few seconds to dry the starch and fix your turned edge in place.

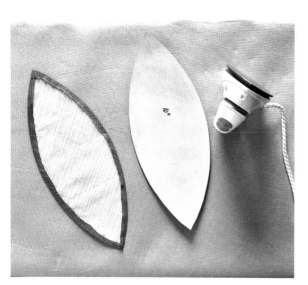

5. When all of the edge has been turned, remove the card template and re-use.

6. Place the prepared appliqué on your chosen background and pin or baste (tack) it in place. Sew in place by hand or machine.

ADDING BORDERS

Quilts often have one or more borders around them. Borders can be simple or complex, plain or fancy, 'whole' or pieced: the choices are endless! Borders can really make a quilt when they are well chosen and well applied. Follow my tips for border success!

1. Keep a sense of scale. A border is usually there to frame and draw attention to the quilt centre, so keep the proportions of the border sympathetic. Frames that are proportionate to the blocks in the centre look pleasing to the eye – so, for example, if the blocks are 10" (25cm) then a 5" (12.5cm) border will inevitably look more 'right' than a 6" (15cm) border. If you're adding multiple borders it's a good idea to keep the total width no bigger than one of the blocks. For example choose 2" (5cm), 6" (16cm) and 2" (5cm) borders for a quilt with 10" (25cm) blocks.

2. Create 'natural-fit' borders for your quilt by using elements from the pieced blocks as a border. For example, in the Scrap Frame quilt (see page 104 and below), I have used the same Flying Geese used in the blocks to create a border. They are the same size as those used in the blocks, so the fit is natural and they are completely in proportion with the rest of the quilt. They enhance rather than overpower the design.

3. Use a multi-coloured border fabric to create 'sense' out of a myriad of scraps. Quilters often find a patterned border fabric first and choose their colours from this, but when we make scrap quilts we inevitably have to work in reverse. Finding a border fabric that is just right can be a challenge, so I prefer to pick the border fabric before the blocks are joined together. That way, if I need to introduce an extra colour or two into the quilt to make the border 'work', I can!

4. Add borders to increase the size of a quilt without having to make a huge number of extra blocks. For example, if you're using 6" (15cm) blocks and you want a 66" x 72" (168 x 183cm) quilt you are going to need to piece 132 blocks. Make that quilt 6" (15cm) bigger on all sides and you'll need either an additional 50 blocks, or simply add a 6" (15cm) border!

5. Use a folded or 'flange' border (see page 29) to add a pop of colour to your quilt. Sometimes that's all that's needed to create harmony in a quilt.

Where a quilt has multiple pieced and plain borders, getting the fit right is essential. Measure carefully, check your seam allowances are correct and pin for perfection!

27

Like a lot of things, there's a right way to add a border and a wrong way... let's look at the wrong ways first.

The very wrong way to add a border

1. Sew a long strip of fabric to the side of the quilt.
2. Chop the ends of the strip off, even with the quilt centre.
3. Hope and pray that the quilt stays square.

Why is this so wrong? Well, the outer edges of a quilt top generally flare out slightly. Fabric can stretch as it's sewn, so the outer edge can become very distorted and will 'ripple' and 'frill' instead of being perfectly straight and square.

The slightly less wrong way to add a border

1. Measure the side of the quilt.
2. Cut a piece of fabric to this length.
3. Sew the strip to the side of your quilt.
4. Repeat on all four sides.

Why is this still a bit wrong? Well, we are assuming that the edges of the quilt are straight and square, and generally they are not. Our borders are still likely to ripple – although not as much as the 'very wrong' way to add a border method.

The right way to add a border

1. Measure through the centre of your quilt top, from top to bottom, and make a note of the measurement.
2. Repeat the measuring process at a quarter and three-quarters along the quilt.
3. Add the measurements together and divide by three; in other words, take several measurements and find the average.
4. Cut two side border pieces to this length.
5. Find the centre of the border and place a pin. Find the quarter positions, too, and again place pins.
6. Find the quarter, half and three-quarter positions on the side of your quilt and match up the pinned border.
7. Match the ends and pin, too.
8. Pin well in between, easing any slight fullness throughout the seam.
9. Sew the border in place.
10. Press the border back, then add the opposite border in the same way.
11. Repeat the measuring process through the width of the quilt and border to find the required length for the remaining two sides.

Yes, it takes longer than methods 1 and 2. Yes, it's worth it!

In this example, I have measured my quilt (in inches) through the centre (1) at 94", at the quarter point (2) at 96" and at the three-quarters point (3) at 95". So the average measurement, and the required length of my side border pieces is 95": 94 + 96 + 95 divided by three.

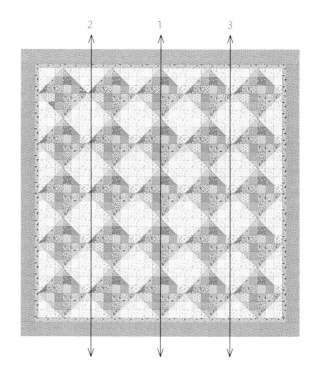

Adding a folded or 'flange' border

1. Measure your quilt for the side outer border pieces and cut those pieces to size. For example, for a 4" (10.2cm) finished border cut two border strips at 4½" (11.4cm) x length of your quilt top and two at 4½" (11.4cm) x width of your quilt top plus the width of the borders.
2. Also cut four strips of your 'flange' fabric to the same length, then fold this narrow strip in half, wrong sides together, and press.
3. Pin and baste (tack) these folded strips to the edges of your quilt, with the raw edges aligned and the folds pointing inwards towards the quilt centre. At the corners, simply overlap the folded strips.
4. Pin your first outer border strip (in this case the 4½"/11.4cm strip) to one side of the quilt, overlapping the folded flange.
5. Sew the border on with a ¼" (6mm) seam.
6. Press the border back to reveal a 4" (10.2cm) finished border with a narrow folded flange captured in the seam.
7. Repeat on the opposite side, and then on the top and bottom edges of the quilt.

A flange is a strip of fabric that goes between the quilt centre and the border. It can be any width – just choose the finished width and double it, then add a ½" (12mm) seam allowance to find the width of the strip you need to cut. For example, for a ¾" (19mm) flange you would double ¾" (19mm). That makes 1½" (3.8cm) and then add ½" (12mm) for seam allowances. So cut strips at 2" (5.1cm) wide by however long your quilt side is.

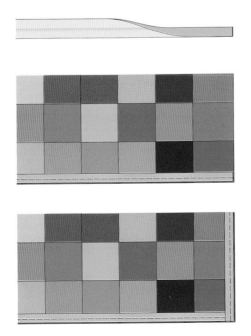

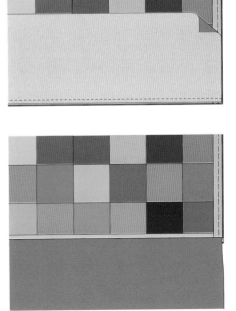

LAYERING

Once your quilt top is completed you're almost ready to layer and quilt... I said almost! Before you layer your quilt top, there are a few jobs to be done.

1. Clip any threads that are hanging loose on the back or front of your quilt top.
2. Make sure that seams are well pressed and are laying flat. If any seams are twisted, unpick the twisted part, flatten and re-sew.
3. Sew around the outer edge of your quilt top about ⅛" (3mm) in from the raw edge to stabilize it.
4. Give your quilt top a final press.

Cut a piece of backing fabric for your quilt. It needs to be at least 2" (5.1cm) bigger on all sides than the quilt top. Piece the backing if necessary to get the required size. Make sure that these seams are pressed open to reduce bulk and avoid a ridge.

Cut a piece of quilt batting (wadding) to the same size as the backing fabric. It's a really good idea to open out your batting 24–48 hours before layering to allow the wrinkles to 'relax'. Just lay it out over a spare bed for a day or so.

1. Lay your backing fabric down, wrong side up. Smooth out and tape at the edges with masking tape.
2. Lay your batting on top and smooth from the centre out to make sure it is flat and wrinkle free.
3. Lay your quilt top on top, right side facing up, centring the top on the batting and backing and placing it 2" (5.1cm) down from the top.
4. Use curved safety pins to hold the layers together. As a general rule I try to make sure there is no more than a fist's width between the pins.

Alternatively use 505 quilt basting spray to temporarily hold the layers of your 'quilt sandwich' together while you quilt. Follow the manufacturer's instructions to do this.

The quilt batting and backing don't need to be cut square at this stage; just make that sure you have at least 2" (5.1cm) extra on all sides.

QUILTING

There's a saying amongst quilters – 'It's not a quilt until it's quilted' – and this is certainly true in my book! A quilt consists of three layers: the top, the backing and a layer of batting (wadding) in between. Machine or hand stitches through all three layers hold them together – this is the 'quilting'.

Your chosen batting will recommend how far apart your lines of stitches need to be in order to hold the quilt together properly, but as a general guide quilting should be evenly spread across the whole quilt surface to be aesthetically pleasing and functional.

Quilting can be done by hand or machine, and nowadays it can also be done by credit card. I shall explain!

Quilting by hand

Using a short 'betweens' (or quilting) needle and a 16" (40cm) length of strong thread, sew a running stitch through the layers of the quilt. Start and finish with a small knot that can be pulled into the middle of the quilt to hide it. Aim to keep your stitches even on the front and back. 'Big stitch' hand quilting is another popular choice and involves using cotton perle thread and a larger than usual running stitch to add decorative hand quilting to certain parts of your quilt.

Quilting by machine

Use a 'walking foot' for straight lines and a 'darning foot' for free-motion swirls, shapes and stipples. Machine quilting can be as simple as sewing slightly to one side of all of the main blocks and pieces in a quilt, or can form an integral part of the overall design. The choices are yours. There are a number of great books specifically on this important skill and it's worth considering this as a separate skill to patchworking.

Quilting by credit card

'Longarm quilting' is a very useful service offered by a number of professionals and is well worth considering if you do not enjoy or are daunted by the task of quilting on your domestic sewing machine. You send the top to a 'longarmer', who then professionally quilts your top for a fee and sends it back to you for binding. Make sure you discuss what you would like before sending your precious top away and follow the longarm quilter's directions for preparation to the letter!

BINDING

I like to bind my quilts with double fold binding cut at 2½" (6.4cm) on the straight of grain.
This gives a sturdy binding and is the most commonly used type of quilting.

1. Measure the four sides of your quilt, add together and add 10" (25.4cm) extra for corners and overlap. Cut strips of fabric from the widthwise or lengthwise grain of your fabric and piece together to give this length. Use straight or diagonal seams and press the seams open to reduce bulk.

2. Fold the binding strip in half to create a strip that is 1¼" (3.2cm) wide with the right sides of the fabric on the outside. Also fold 1" (2.5cm) in on the lead end and press to neaten it.

3. Starting on the right side of the quilt and approximately 6" (15cm) down from a corner, pin the neatened end of the binding to the raw edge of the quilt.

4. Using a ¼" (6mm) seam allowance and starting approximately 3" (7.6cm) down from the neatened edge, sew the binding to the first side of the quilt, finishing exactly ¼" (6mm) from the corner and backstitching to secure your thread.

5. Take the quilt out from under your machine and clip your threads.

6. With the newly bound edge of your quilt at the top and the next edge to be bound on the right-hand side, fold your binding strip up until it is in line with the next edge to be bound.

7. Fold the binding back down on itself and align the raw edges of the binding with the raw edge of the quilt. Pin at the corner.

8. Start sewing ¼" (6mm) in from the edge of the quilt and sew with a ¼" (6mm) seam until you get to ¼" (6mm) off the next corner. Backstitch, remove your quilt from the machine and clip the threads. Repeat for each side of the quilt.

9. When you get back to the first edge, make the last corner and sew approximately 2" (5cm) down. Backstitch and clip threads.

10. Trim the end of your binding strip, allowing about 1" (2.5cm) to tuck inside the neatened lead edge. Pin in place and sew the remaining binding in place.

Once the binding has been machine sewn to the front of your quilt, you can turn the folded edge to the back of your quilt and slip stitch it in place by hand. It's a fairly slow process to do well, but you will be left with an immaculate binding that will really finish your quilts to perfection!

USEFUL EQUIPMENT

If you're already a quilter, then you will almost certainly have everything you need to start your scrap quilting adventure. If this is your first foray into patchwork, then you are in for a treat! You will need some basic equipment. Don't be put off by the list – these things can last a lifetime!

The hard stuff

SEWING MACHINE You'll need a sewing machine that sews a good straight stitch and for the majority of quiltmaking it need be nothing more complex than that! A zigzag stitch and blanket stitch are both useful for machine appliqué.

SCISSORS For cutting both fabric and paper. I like a large pair of shears for cutting yardage and small pointed embroidery scissors for cutting out appliqués and finer detail.

THREAD SNIPS Because nothing dulls a pair of scissors' blades like snipping thread!

PINS I like fine, long pins for piecing and shorter, fine pins for appliqué. Lace, lingerie or bridal pins are most suitable.

HAND SEWING NEEDLES I like milliners/sharps for appliqué and hand sewing binding. For hand quilting I use a 'between'.

MACHINE NEEDLES I love microtex needles for my machine piecing, appliqué and quilting and generally use a 75 for everything if I can get away with it. Use a larger needle if you are having issues with thread breakage and, of course, match your needle to your thread type, particularly if you use embroidery or metallic threads. Change your needles regularly. I recommend every 6–8 hours of sewing time or before if you notice skipped or poorly formed stitches or the needle is bent.

ROTARY CUTTER, RULER AND SELF-HEALING MAT The holy trinity of cutting! Always use these three items together for accuracy and safety. I like a trigger grip cutter, a 6" x 24" (15.2 x 61cm) Perspex ruler and an A2 cutting mat.

OTHER RULERS A 12" (30.5cm) or 15" (38.1cm) square is wonderful for cutting larger pieces easily and quickly and for trimming quilts after quilting. A smaller rotary cutting ruler, say 6" x 12" (15.2 x 30.5cm) or 3" x 12" (7.6 x 30.5cm), is useful for cutting smaller pieces and trimming.

TEMPLATE PLASTIC Perfect for cutting templates for curved shapes, appliqués and for those who prefer to cut with scissors. Cereal box cardboard is another option, particularly if only a few shapes are required.

DIE CUTTING MACHINE AND DIES Cut accurately, quickly and without the associated hand and arm strain of scissors and rotary cutting methods by using a die cutting system..

CURVED SAFETY PINS Ideal for pinning the layers of a quilt together in preparation for quilting. Buy in bulk, as many hundreds will be needed to pin baste a large quilt.

505 QUILT BASTING SPRAY A temporary adhesive spray used to hold the layers of a quilt together, eliminating the need for pinning or traditional thread basting (tacking). Always use in a well-ventilated room or outdoors, and away from pets.

The soft stuff

FABRIC For quilting I generally only use 100% cotton quilt weight fabric. It's easy to piece, presses well and is available in a fabulous array of colours and patterns. I don't mix fabrics of different weights and types in a quilt, but if you want to it's a good idea to fuse lightweight interfacing to the back of the lighter fabrics in order to 'bring them up' to the same weight as the heavier fabrics. Do this also if you are mixing fabrics with stretch.

Some quilters like to pre-wash their fabrics, others do not. I'm in the 'not' camp and prefer to wash my finished quilts. This way any shrinkage is spread through the finished quilt and lends my quilts a gently 'wrinkled' look, which I like. I always put half a dozen colour-catching sheets into the wash and use a 30°C cycle and colour liquid. Follow these same guidelines for pre-washing fabrics, but always test fabrics for colourfastness before washing.

BACKING FABRIC I like to use a fabric of similar quality and weight to the fabrics used on the front of my quilt. This generally means that I have to piece my backings to get the required size, although extra-wide quilt backing fabrics are available. Piece your backing with a ½" (12mm) seam allowance and press seams open to distribute the bulk.

THREAD I like to use pure cotton thread for my piecing and I use a neutral grey/beige shade which blends with pretty much everything. For machine quilting I like a cotton or cotton polyester mix, although rayon, metallic thread and silk are all possible.

FUSIBLE WEB A fine web of glue adhered to a paper backing used for fusible appliqué. Various weights are available depending on the results you want.

FUSIBLE AND SEW-IN INTERFACING A non-woven 'fabric' that is bonded or stitched to lighter-weight fabrics in order to make them heavier or more stable. Can also be used as a foundation in place of paper for foundation piecing.

QUILT BATTING (WADDING) There is far more choice in quilt battings now than there was when I started quilting. In addition to pure cotton or polyester, you will now find silk, bamboo and wool as well as blends of some of these fibres. My general preference is for a pure cotton

or a cotton and polyester blend (80/20 or 70/30), which has slightly more loft (thickness) and shows off machine or hand quilting better than the very thin cotton battings. Wool is a great choice in temperate climates and bamboo or recycled polyester is a good choice and an 'eco-friendly' alternative.

100 QUILTS

SCRAPPY SIXTEEN PATCH

Sometimes the simplest designs work the best and my Scrappy Sixteen Patch certainly gives a lot of bang for your buck! The key is to use lots of intense colour, one print and one wildly clashing solid per block. Individual blocks might make your hair curl, but when they are all joined together your colour confidence will pay huge dividends!

SUGGESTED LAYOUT

For my quilt, I made eighty-one Scrappy Sixteen Patch blocks and sewed them together in nine rows of nine. I had a collection of print and solid 10" (25.4cm) squares (a layer cake). I used one print and one solid layer cake square to make two finished sixteen-patch blocks. The quilt finishes at 72" x 72" (182.8 x 182.8cm).

For one block you will need

Finished block size: 8" (20.3cm) square

- 5" x 10" (12.7 x 25.4cm) scrap of vibrant print
- 5" x 10" (12.7 x 25.4cm) scrap of vibrant solid

Assembling the block

1. Cut each scrap into two 2½" x 10" (6.4 x 25.4cm) strips.
2. Rearrange the strips so that you have print, solid, print, solid. Sew the rows together, matching the ends carefully.
3. Press your seams in one direction, then cut the pieced panel into four segments, each 2½" x 8½" (6.4 x 21.6cm).
4. Rearrange the segments to create a checkerboard, then sew the strips back together.

Making pairs of scrappy blocks, with the same colourations, is a good way to achieve balance in a quilt. Whereas one block might look a little odd and 'stick out', adding its twin on the opposite side of the quilt can create a sense of harmony.

STRING SWIRL

What happens when a hurricane blows through your scrap pile? You get String Swirl, a dazzling twister of a quilt! Use your thinnest strips and tiny scraps to make this easy block.

For one block you will need
Finished block size:
16" (40.7cm) square
- Strips and scraps in a mixture of lights, mediums and darks. Strips can be as narrow as ½" (12mm) and as wide as 3" (7.6cm)

Assembling the block
1. Start with a small square or five-sided shape in the centre. Sew a strip to one side, and trim the edges even with the centre.
2. Continue to add strips to the sides, working in a clockwise direction. Trim the sides even as you go, but try to avoid 'squaring up' the block until you have finished. Keep going until the piece measures approximately 17" x 17" (43.2 x 43.2cm). Trim the block to 16½" x 16½" (42 x 42cm).

I often add rather than take away colours that don't appear to work at first. More is more!

SUGGESTED LAYOUT

My virtual quilt uses thirteen full blocks, eight half blocks (for the setting triangles) and four quarter blocks for the corners. To make the setting triangles, sew four 18" x 18" (45.7 x 45.7cm) String Swirl blocks, cut them in half diagonally, then trim to size after they have been sewn into the quilt top. Make another 18" x 18" (45.7 x 45.7cm) String Swirl block and cut it diagonally into four for the corner triangles. Trim the quilt top centre to 67¾" (172cm) square, then add borders. I added a ¼" (6mm) wide flange border, a 1" (2.5cm) finished border and the binding for a quilt that finishes at approximately 70" x 70" (177.8 x 177.8cm).

FLOCK OF BIRDS

A flock of birds in soft shades of blush pink and raspberry flies over fields of gold in this sweet and simple wall quilt. If your stash is larger, dig deep and multiply the number of blocks for a quilt that's the perfect size for you.

SUGGESTED LAYOUT

In my virtual quilt, I have sewn sixteen blocks together, turning the blocks so that the light gold and dark gold half square triangle units (HSTs) come together. Bind with a dark raspberry pink print. The finished quilt is 36" x 36" (91.4 x 91.4cm).

I like to make HSTs slightly larger than I need, then trim them back to the correct size after piecing. If you want to do likewise, leave the squares at 2" (5.1cm) and 4" (10.2cm), piece the HST units, then press, and trim to 1½" (3.8cm) square or 3½" (8.9cm) square, making sure you align the centre diagonal carefully.

For one block you will need

Finished block size: 9" (22.9cm) square

- Nine different pink scraps, each approximately 2" (5.1cm) square
- Nine different light gold scraps, each approximately 2" (5.1cm) square
- One pink scrap approximately 4" (10.2cm) square
- One light gold scrap approximately 4" (10.2cm) square
- One dark gold scrap approximately 4" (10.2cm) square

Note

I've used more than nine pinks and golds and I'd recommend you do the same if making multiple blocks.

Assembling the block

1. Cut the 2" (5.1cm) pink and light gold scraps into squares each 1⅞" x 1⅞" (4.8 x 4.8cm). Pair them right sides together, one gold and one pink, and mark one diagonal with a pencil. Sew ¼" (6mm) either side of the pencil line, then cut apart on the drawn line to create a total of eighteen half square triangles (HSTs). See also page 19.
2. Sew nine pink/gold HST units together as shown to make unit 1. Make two.
3. Cut the 4" (10.2cm) pink, light gold and dark gold scraps into squares each 3⅞" x 3⅞" (9.8cm), then cut each square in half on the diagonal to yield a total of six triangles.
4. Sew one dark gold and one light gold triangle together. Sew one light gold and one pink triangle together. (You will have two triangles left over.)
5. Sew the large half square triangles and unit 1s together as shown to make the block.

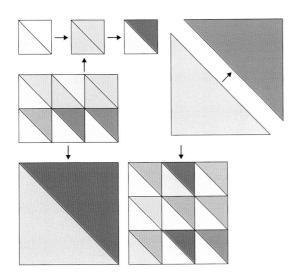

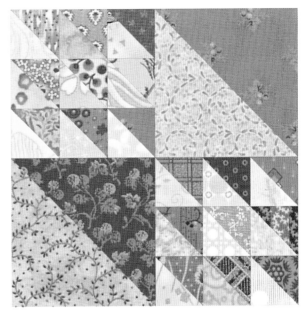

STRINGS

This is a great quilt for using up all those thin strips and offcuts of binding left over from other projects. You can follow my instructions to the letter or vary the width of the strips to your heart's content, but don't go thinner than ¾" (19mm) cut or wider than about 2½" (6.4cm).

SUGGESTED LAYOUT
In my virtual quilt, I used a variety of brown, tan, rust and blue strips. I made a total of thirty blocks and sewed them together in five rows of six to make a quilt centre that measures 50½" x 60½" (128.2 x 153.7cm). I added a narrow ½" (12mm) finished border all around, then a binding in a blue print.

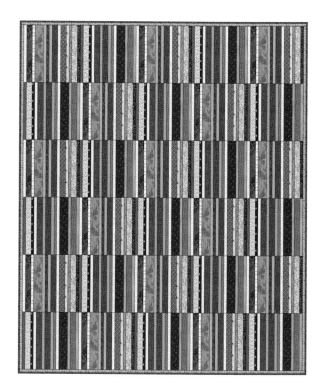

When joining lots of strips, it's a good idea to alternate the direction you join them in. This helps to keep the strips 'straight' and avoid bowing.

For one block you will need
Finished block size: 10" (25.4cm) square
- A selection of strips of fabric, as follows:
  nine 1" x 11" (2.5 x 28cm) strips, three 1½" x 11" (3.8 x 28cm) strips and one 2" x 11" (5.1 x 28cm) strip

Assembling the block
1. Sew the strips together, matching the ends neatly. Vary the placement of the thinner and thicker strips.
2. Press the block carefully, then trim to 10½" x 10½" (26.7 x 26.7cm).

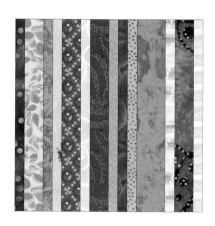

STAIRWAY

Choose your brightest scraps to create a dazzling stairway in this super-easy and quick-to-make quilt. This quilt will put a huge dent in your scrap basket and the blocks fly together with such ease that you might just be tempted to make two! I've used a consistent light background fabric throughout, but you could easily use a variety of creams, tan and ivories for even more scrap charm.

SUGGESTED LAYOUT

In my virtual quilt, I have made a total of forty-nine blocks and sewn them together in seven rows of seven. The finished quilt is 84" x 84" (213.3 x 213.3cm), but is a cinch to make in other sizes.

If your scraps don't 'match' my directions, adapt the pattern! If you have a huge collection of 2½" (6.4cm) strips you can still make this. Cut rectangles at 2½" x 4½" (6.4 x 11.4cm) and proceed as in the instructions. Your finished block will be 8" x 8" (20.3 x 20.3cm); for a quilt measuring 88" x 88" (223.5 x 223.5cm), you will need a total of 121 blocks.

For one block you will need
Finished block size: 12" (30.5cm) square
- Four 3½" x 6½" (8.9 x 16.5cm) strips of bright scraps
- Four 3½" x 6½" (8.9 x 16.5cm) strips of cream print scraps

Assembling the block
1. Sew one cream and one bright scrap print together along the 6½" (16.5cm) length. Press the seams towards the darker fabric. Make four in total.
2. Sew the four units together as shown.

CHECKERBOARD CABIN

Take a humble Log Cabin block to a whole new level by starting with a checkerboard centre. There's something wonderfully grounding about a black-and-white check and simple elements like this can help to tame your wildest prints!

SUGGESTED LAYOUT

For my virtual quilt I have pieced sixteen Checkerboard Cabin blocks and sewn them together in four rows of four. A 1" (2.5cm) finished border all around makes a quilt that is 50" x 50" (127 x 127cm) – perfect as a lap or throw quilt.

For one block you will need

Finished block size: 12" (30.5cm) square

- Eight black or dark brown print 1½" (3.8cm) squares
- Eight white solid 1½" (3.8cm) squares
- Sixteen assorted print strips 1½" (3.8cm) wide and ranging from 4½" (11.4cm) up to 12½" (31.7cm) long

Cutting the strips to the exact size for the log cabins may take a little time, but it's worth it! The blocks will be super accurate and easy to assemble. Don't be tempted to just sew a long strip on each side and trim as you go. The edges tend to grow and bow outward, and the blocks will turn out to be less accurate!

Assembling the block

1. Sew the black/brown and white 1½" (3.8cm) squares together in pairs, sew the pairs into a row of four, and finally sew the rows together to make the checkerboard centre. Press the seams towards the black/brown fabrics.

2. Starting with a 4½" (11.4cm) assorted print strip, sew this strip to one side of the checkerboard. Add a 5½" (14cm) strip to the next side, another 5½" (14cm) strip to the next side and finally a 6½" (16.5cm) strip to the fourth side. This completes round one.

3. Round two is similar: add a 6½" (16.5cm) strip, a 7½" (19cm) strip, another 7½" (19cm) strip and finally an 8½" (21.6cm) strip to the fourth side. This completes round two.

4. For round three use strips of 8½" (21.6cm), 9½" (24.1cm), 9½" (24.1cm) and 10½" (26.7cm).

5. For round four use strips of 10½" (26.7cm), 11½" (29.2cm), 11½" (29.2cm) and 12½" (31.7cm).

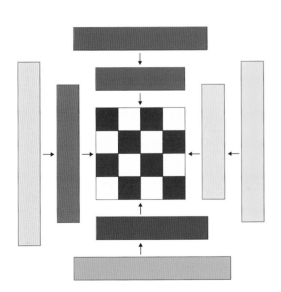

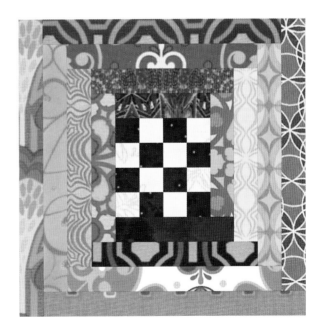

STARS AND CUBES

Two easy to piece blocks go together to create a quilt that is much more complex than it looks. I've used a selection of small scraps and teamed them with a collection of indigo fat quarters. Most of us can't resist buying those cuts of our favourite fabrics and they work extremely well for scrap quilts so long as you have a reasonable collection of them... that sounds like an excuse for a shopping trip to me!

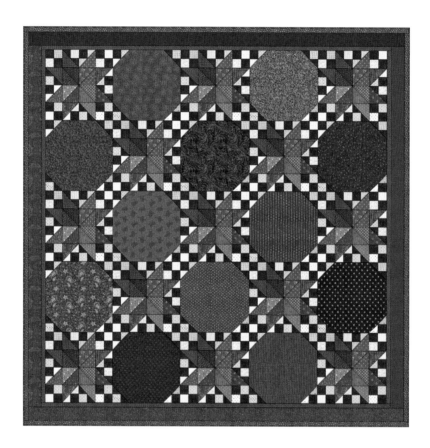

SUGGESTED LAYOUT

For my virtual quilt I have made thirteen Star blocks and twelve Checkered Snowball blocks and sewn them together in five rows of five. I added a 1" (2.5cm) finished border in red, a 3" (7.6cm) finished border in blue and a final 1" (2.5cm) finished border in red. The quilt finishes at 70" x 70" (177.8 x 178.8cm).

For one Star block you will need

Finished block size: 12" (30.5cm) square

- Sixteen assorted red 4⅞" x 4⅞" (12.4 x 12.4cm) squares cut once on the diagonal to yield thirty-two half square triangles (this gives you enough for two blocks)
- Twelve black or very dark brown 2½" (6.4cm) squares
- Twelve cream print 2½" (6.4cm) squares
- Four black or very dark brown 2⅞" (7.3cm) squares cut once on the diagonal (yields eight triangles)
- Four cream print 2⅞" (7.3cm) squares cut once on the diagonal (yields eight triangles)

Assembling the Star block

1. Sew eight of the assorted red scrap half square triangles to create the centre pinwheel unit.
2. Sew two black/brown and two cream 2½" (6.4cm) squares together to make a corner four patch unit. Make four.
3. Sew two black/brown triangles and one cream 2½" (6.4cm) square together, as shown, then sew to one of the remaining red triangles. Make four.
4. Sew two cream triangles and one black/brown square together in the same way as step 3, then sew to one of the remaining red triangles. Make four.
5. Assemble the block as shown.

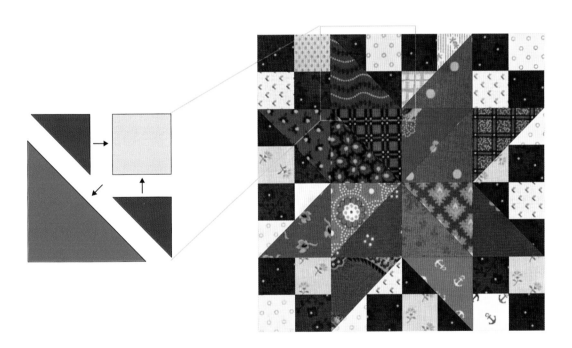

For a great scrappy look use four different, but similar prints for the four sides of the blue border. It adds a touch of 'make do' to this classic scrap quilt.

STARS AND CUBES

For one Checkered Snowball block you will need

Finished block size: 12" (30.5cm) square

- One 16½" (42cm) square of indigo print
- Two black or very dark brown 2½" (6.4cm) squares
- Two cream print 2½" (6.4cm) squares
- Two black or very dark brown 2⅞" (7.3cm) squares cut once on the diagonal (yields four triangles)
- Two cream print 2⅞" (7.3cm) squares cut once on the diagonal (yields four triangles)

Assembling the Checkered Snowball block

1. Use the trimming template on page 225 to trim the corners off the indigo blue square, as shown below.
2. Sew two cream triangles and one black/brown square together. Make two and sew to opposite corners of the trimmed indigo square. Fold back and press.
3. Sew two black/brown triangles and one cream print square together. Make two and sew to the remaining corners of the indigo square. Fold back and press.

Trimming template

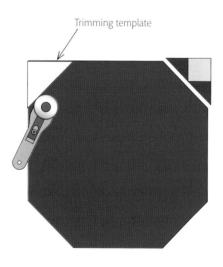

STRIPPING

I based this quilt on a vintage one I saw at a show. The original had clearly helped its maker clear out their scrap basket and this modern version will do the same for you. Use your favourite colour palette or throw everything you have at this scrappy beauty.

SUGGESTED LAYOUT

For my virtual quilt I have made nine Stripping blocks and sewn them in a three rows of three for a finished wall hanging that measures 54" x 54" (137.2 x 137.2cm).

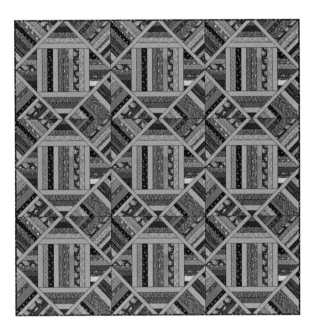

For one block you will need

Finished block size: 18" (45.7cm) square
- A good supply of brown, tan and blue strips
- 10" (25cm) of gold tone on tone

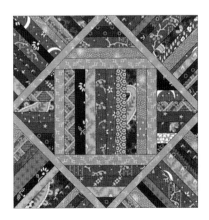

Assembling the block

1. Download and print (see page 224 for link) or photocopy one copy of Stripping foundation A, two copies of foundation B, two copies of foundation C and four copies of foundation D (page 224).
2. Following the general instructions for paper foundation piecing (page 21), piece the block units in numerical order, trimming the seam allowances as you go. Sew the units together.

LIPSTICK AND POLISH

These paper-pieced blocks, featuring tubes of lipstick and bottles of glossy nail polish, are so much fun to piece and the level of accuracy needed is easy to achieve using this very useful method. I made this quilt for my Mom, Rosemary, who would feel totally naked without her lipstick and polish!

SUGGESTED LAYOUT

For my quilt I made a total of sixteen Lipstick and Polish blocks in various glamorous shades. I used solid fabrics throughout but tone on tone prints, batiks and prints that read as 'solid' would work equally well. I added 1" (2.5cm) finished sashing between the blocks and a 2" (5.1cm) finished border in turquoise and a final dark grey binding. My quilt finished at 45" x 45" (114 x 114cm) – perfect for the wall.

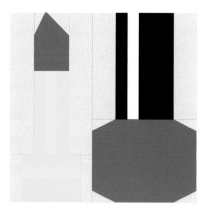

For one block you will need

Finished block size: 9" (22.9cm) square

- 8" (20.3cm) square of bright solid for the lipstick and polish 'colour'
- Scraps of light and medium gold, black and white.
- Scraps of one background fabric (I used a light pearl grey)

Assembling the block

1. Download and print (see page 224 for link) or photocopy one copy each of Lipstick and Polish foundations A, B, C and D (page 224).
2. Following the general instructions for paper foundation piecing (page 21), piece the block units in numerical order, trimming seam allowances as you go. Sew the units together.

This would make a great quilt to give as a gift for a bride-to-be with the names of girlfriends embroidered on each bottle of polish.

10 JEWEL

Pastel backgrounds meet rich jewel tones for a block that almost reflects light! This is a great opportunity to use scraps of similar hue but varying value (lightness or darkness) and would make a wonderful quilt or wall hanging for a teenager's room.

For one block you will need

Finished block size: 9" (22.9cm) square

- Five different scraps of the same colour in various values, from very light to very dark
- One background fabric

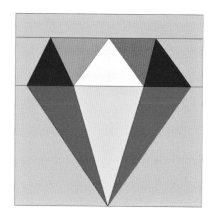

Assembling the block

1. Download and print (see page 224 for link) or photocopy one copy each of Jewel foundation A and B (page 225).
2. Cut one strip 1½" x 9½" (3.8 x 24.1cm) from the background fabric and set aside.
3. Following the general instructions for paper foundation piecing (page 21), piece the block units in numerical order paying careful attention to the placement of lights, mediums and darks, and trimming the seam allowances as you go.
4. Sew foundation A to the top of foundation B.
5. Sew the 1½" x 9½" (3.8 x 24.1cm) strip of background fabric to the top of the block.

If you're unsure about the value (lightness/darkness) of a fabric, simply photocopy or scan and print the fabric in greyscale. The value will be obvious!

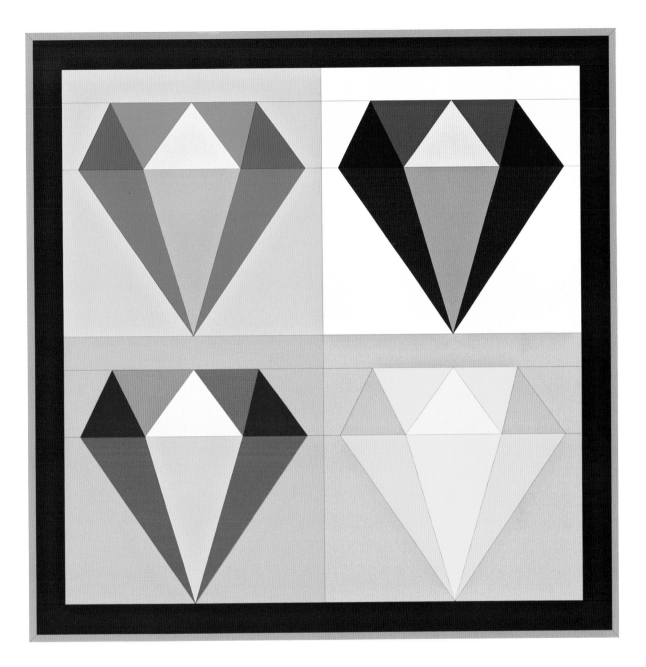

SUGGESTED LAYOUT

For my virtual quilt I have pieced
four Jewel blocks: a ruby, an emerald,
a sapphire and a canary diamond.
I've joined the blocks edge to edge,
with a 1" (2.5cm) finished border, for a
wall hanging that finishes at 20" x 20"
(50.5 x 50.5cm) .

ICE CREAM CONE

I scream, you scream, we all scream for an ice cream cone quilt... or something like that! I just love piecing novelty blocks and paper piecing is the perfect method for weird and oddly shaped pieces. Dig into your stash and find anything that remotely resembles a flavour of ice cream, from chocolate and mint to vanilla, strawberry and peach. Make up a few flavours of your own and piece this fun and fruity little number!

For one block you will need

Finished block size: 9" x 11" (22.9 x 28in)

- Three different scraps for the 'ice cream' approximately 3" x 9" (7.6 x 22.9cm) and smaller
- 7" x 5" (17.8 x 12.7cm) rectangle of brown/gold for the cone
- One background fabric (one fat quarter)

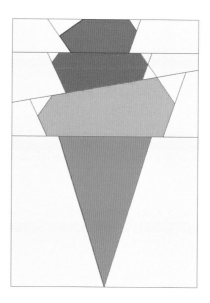

Assembling the block

1. Download and print (see page 224 for link) or photocopy one each of Ice Cream Cone foundations A, B, C, D and E (page 226).

2. Following the general instructions for paper foundation piecing (page 21), piece the units in numerical order, trimming the seam allowances as you go, then sew the units together.

Flip some of the blocks or sub-units to create a quilt that has more visual interest. Simply scan the foundation into your computer, flip the image to the left or right and then save and print.

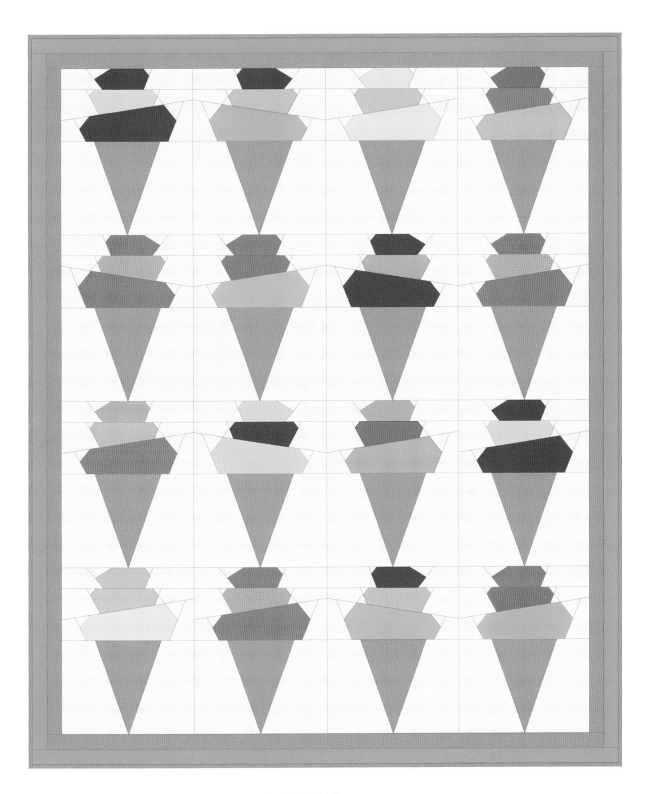

SUGGESTED LAYOUT

For my virtual quilt I set sixteen blocks together in four rows of four. I added borders in gold and turquoise, both 1" (2.5cm) finished, for a quilt that finishes at 40" x 48" (101.6 x 122cm).

12 WOVEN RIBBONS

Use leftover 2½" (6.4cm) strips, a jelly roll, or cut strips from your larger scraps and piece this bold and beautiful quilt. Half a jelly roll would be enough, with background fabric, to make this quilt. If your strips are narrower, follow the general instructions, but add more strips to make the block up to 10½" (26.7cm).

For one block you will need

Finished block size:

10" (25.4cm) square

- Five assorted teal/turquoise strips, each 2½" (6.4cm) x 10½" (26.7cm)
- Two solid black 3½" (8.9cm) squares

Assembling the block

1. Sew the five teal strips together to make a 10½" (26.7cm) pieced square. Press the seams one way.
2. Mark one diagonal on the back of both black squares.
3. Place a square on two opposing sides of the pieced square, as shown, right sides together.
4. Sew on the marked line. Trim the excess away, leaving a ¼" (6mm) seam allowance. Press the black triangle corners back. See also page 20.

Set your seams by running an iron along the length of the seam while the right sides are still together. This bit of heat helps to 'set' the stitches and tighten them slightly for a firmer, more durable seam. Once the seams are set, you can press the seams to either side.

SUGGESTED LAYOUT

For my virtual quilt I made sixteen blocks and sewed them together in four rows of four. I added two 1" (2.5cm) finished borders in black and set a ¼" (6mm) flange between them (see page 29). The finished quilt measures 44" x 44" (111.7 x 111.7cm).

EVERY BIT (1)

Who doesn't like to get every bit of value out of their fabrics? This quilt block uses even the tiniest scraps to ensure that your stash is busted and your quilt sparkles with visual interest.

For one block you will need
Finished block size:
16" (40.7cm) square
- Scraps of various golds, tans and blues

Assembling the block

1. From the various blue scraps cut five 4½" (11.4cm) squares for the block centre and corners. From the various blues also cut four 2½" (6.4cm) squares and three 5¼" (13.3cm) squares, which you should then cut on both diagonals to yield eight triangles.

2. From the various tan fabrics, cut four 2⅞" (7.3cm) squares and cut each on one diagonal to yield eight triangles. Also from various tan prints, cut two 5¼" (13.3cm) squares and cut on both diagonals to yield eight triangles.

3. From the various gold fabrics, cut a total of thirty-two 1½" x 2½" (3.8 x 6.4cm) rectangles.

4. Sew four assorted gold 1½" x 2½" (3.8 x 6.4cm) rectangles together, along the long edges. Make a total of eight units like this.

5. Sew them together with the 4½" (11.4cm) blue squares and the 2½" (6.4cm) blue squares to make the corner units.

6. Use the remaining blue and tan triangles to piece the Hourglass and Flying Geese units, as shown.

7. Sew the units into rows and finally sew the rows together.

To make construction of the sashing faster, you can strip piece sixteen 1½" (3.8cm) strips of various gold fabrics. Once the panel is pieced, cut it into 2½" (6.4cm) wide segments. Each segment will make the whole sashing.

SUGGESTED LAYOUT

For my virtual quilt I have set sixteen blocks together
in four rows of four with pieced sashing in between.
The pieced sashing is made up of sixteen 1½" x 2½" (3.8 x
6.4cm) rectangles of various gold prints. The cornerstones
are in various blues and are cut at 2½" (6.4cm) square. A final
2" (5.1cm) border in blue makes a quilt that is 78" x 78"
(198 x 198cm).

EVERY BIT (2)

A simpler block than Every Bit (1) but still using smaller scraps to make a shape that would, in the traditional version of this block, be made up of one strip of fabric. Strip piecing the rectangular units will speed up the construction.

For one block you will need

Finished block size:
16" (40.7cm) square

- Four assorted dark gold scraps, each 4⅞" (12.4cm) square, cut once on the diagonal (yields eight triangles)
- Four assorted tan/cream scraps, each 4⅞" (12.4cm) square, cut once on the diagonal (yields eight triangles)
- Sixteen assorted blue scraps, each 2½" x 4½" (6.4cm x 11.4cm) (alternatively sew four longer strips – each 2½"/6.4cm wide – together and cross cut into 2½"/6.4cm x 8½"/21.6cm segments)

Assembling the block

1. Sew the gold and tan or cream triangles together to make a total of eight half square triangle (HST) units.
2. Sew four of the HST units together to make the centre unit.
3. Sew four of the 2½" x 4½" (6.4 x 11.4cm) blue rectangles together, as shown. Make four of these units in total.
4. Sew the units together to make the block, as shown.

If piecing all those tiny scraps for the border is too daunting, you could always use 2½" x 4½" (6.4 x 11.4cm) pieces, just as you did in the blocks.

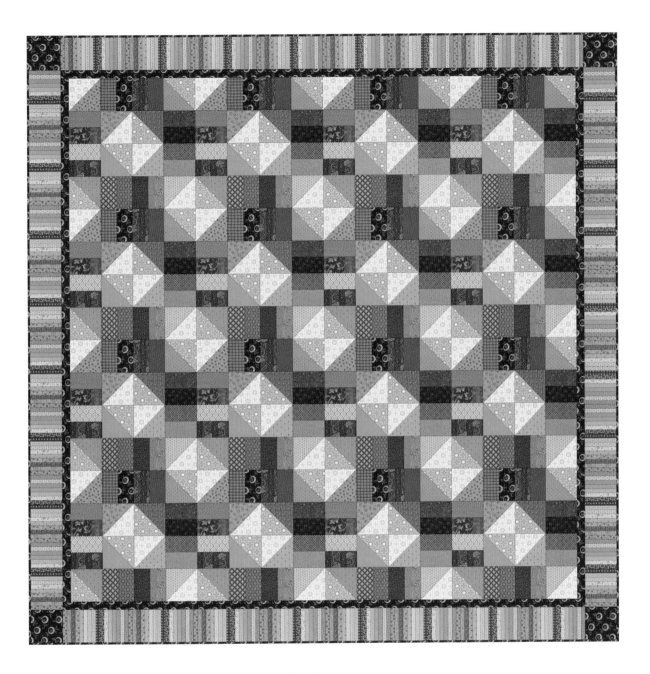

SUGGESTED LAYOUT

For my virtual quilt I have set sixteen blocks together in four rows of four. I added a 1" (2.5cm) finished blue border and then strip pieced the final 4" (10.2cm) wide finished border from 1" x 4½" (2.5 x 11.4cm) cut pieces of assorted golds with 4½" (11.4cm) blue corner squares. The border strips finish at ½" (12mm) wide and really do use up the tiniest of scraps! The quilt finishes at 74" x 74" (188 x 188cm).

SUMMER'S END

Sometimes a really strong print is needed to pull together a whole host of disparate scraps and contain them. That's just what I did here with Summer's End, a gloriously traditional mix of Flying Geese and half square triangles.

For one block you will need
Finished block size:
10" (25.4cm) square

- One 7" (17.8cm) square of main print
- One 2½" (6.4cm) square of green print for block centre
- Twelve 1⅞" (4.8cm) squares of green scraps for the HST units
- Twelve 1⅞" (4.8cm) squares of cream scraps for the HST units
- Twelve 1⅞" (4.8cm) squares of green scraps for the Flying Geese units
- Three 3¼" (8.3cm) squares of cream scraps for the Flying Geese units
- Four 1½" (3.8cm) squares of cream scraps for the corners
- Four 1½" x 2½" (6.4cm) rectangles of cream scraps

Assembling the block

1. Cut the main print square into four to give four 3½" (8.9cm) squares.
2. Pair up the cream and green 1⅞" (4.8cm) squares and make a total of 24 half square triangle (HST) units (see page 19).
3. Make a total of twelve Flying Geese units using the 3¼" (8.3cm) cream squares and the twelve remaining 1⅞" (4.8cm) squares of green scraps (three sets using the no-waste Flying Geese method – see page 20).
4. Sew the units together as shown and then sew the rows together. Press the seams away from the dark fabrics wherever possible.

SUGGESTED LAYOUT

For my virtual quilt I have set sixteen blocks together
with pieced sashing. The sashing is based on the Flying
Geese units used in the blocks. Each piece of sashing
consists of ten Flying Geese units, each finishing at 1" x 2"
(2.5 x 5.1cm). The cornerstones finish at 2" (5.1cm) square
and are cut from the main print. I've added borders that
finish at 1" (2.5cm), 6" (15.2cm) and finally at 1" (2.5cm) for
a quilt that measures 66" x 66" (167.6 x 167.6cm).

16 STREAK O' LIGHTNING

Give this traditional block a modern new look with a larger than usual scale, a collection of vibrant solids and bold black-and-white centres. Jelly roll strips are perfect for this project or dig into your stash and cut your own 2½" (6.4cm) strips of all your favourite prints and make a more traditional version. Cutting the 'logs' to length before piecing ensures accurate blocks!

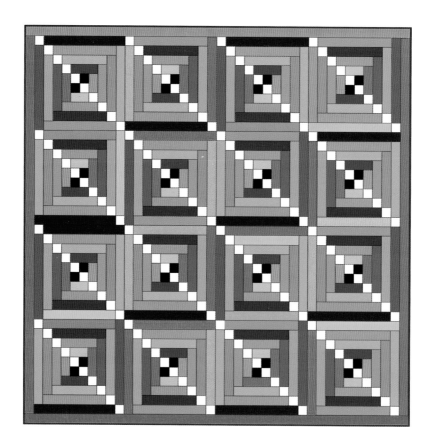

SUGGESTED LAYOUT

For my virtual quilt I made sixteen blocks and set them together in a traditional 'streak o' lightning' set, but you can have lots of fun creating other patterns with this very versatile block. A 2" (5.1cm) finished border, made up of four different fabrics, adds to the scrappy look for a finished quilt that measure 84" x 84" (213.3 x 213.3cm), great for a double bed.

For one block you will need

Finished block size: 20" (50.8cm) square

- Two 2½" (6.4cm) squares of black solid
- Ten 2½" (6.4cm) squares of white solid
- Sixteen 2½" (6.4cm) strips of bold solids in lengths ranging from 4½" (11.4cm) up to 18½" (47cm)

Assembling the block

1. Sew one black and one white 2½" (6.4cm) square together, make two. Join the units to make the centre four-patch unit.
2. Sew a 2½" x 4½" (6.4 x 11.4cm) bright solid log to one side of the four patch.
3. Join a 2½" (6.4cm) white square to the end of another 2½" x 4½" (6.4 x 11.4cm) bright solid, then join this unit to the second side of the four patch.
4. Join a 2½" (6.4cm) x 6½" (6.4 x 16.5cm) bright solid log to the third side of the four patch.
5. Join a 2½" (6.4cm) white square to the end of a 2½" x 6½" (6.4 x 16.5cm) bright solid log, then join this unit to the fourth side of the four patch. Round one is complete.
6. Complete rounds two, three and four in a similar fashion. Each log is 2" (5.1cm) longer than the one it is stitched to.

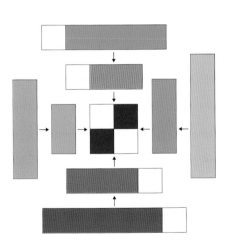

ROADS AND CROSSINGS

Grab your stash of black-and-white prints and a whole host of bright scraps and make this vibrant quilt. Strip piecing speeds up the process and the uniform sizes of strips and squares will help to tame even the most unlikely scraps into a quilt of beauty.

For one block you will need
Finished block size:
12" (30.5cm) square

- Eight strips of black-and-white prints, each 1½" x 5" (3.8 x 12.7cm)
- Four strips of bright print scraps, each 1½" x 10" (3.8 x 25.4cm)
- Four strips of black-and-white prints each 1½" x 13" (3.8 x 33cm)
- Four strips of bright print scraps each 1½" x 13"(3.8 x 33cm)
- One white-and-black polka dot scrap 1½" x 10" (3.8 x 25.4cm)
- Four 2½" x 2½" (6.4 x 6.4cm) squares of black-and-white polka dot print
- One 1½" x 1½" (3.8 x 3.8cm) black print square

Assembling the block

1. Cut each of the 1½" x 10" (3.8 x 25.4cm) bright print scraps in half to make two strips, each 1½" x 5" (3.8 x 12.7cm). Keep them in pairs. To each pair of bright print strips add two of the black-and-white 1½" x 5" (3.8 x 12.7cm) strips. Sew the four strips together, alternating the colours. Press the seams and then trim the unit to 4½" x 4½" (11.4 x 11.4cm). Make four units.

2. Take one bright print 13" (33cm) strip and one black-and-white 13" (33cm) strip and cut them in half (1½" x 6½"/3.8 x 16.5cm). Sew the four strips together, alternating the colours. Press the seams them cut a total of four segments, each 1½" x 4½" (3.8 x 11.4cm). Rejoin the segments to make a sixteen-patch unit as shown. Make four units.

3. Cut the white-and-black polka dot strip into four pieces (1½" x 2½"/3.8 x 6.4cm). Sew the black-and-white and white-and-black polka dot prints together to make the centre unit, as shown.

4. Sew the units together in rows and finally sew the rows together.

SUGGESTED LAYOUT

For my virtual quilt I made a total of thirty blocks and set them together in a six rows of five, separated by sashing finishing at 1" (2.5cm). I used a black and white 'typography' print for a very modern look. The cornerstones are in the same black-and-white polka dot print from the centre units of the blocks. They finish at 1" (2.5cm) square. There is a final 1" (2.5cm) finished border, making the quilt 66" x 79" (167.6 x 200.6cm) – perfect for a single bed.

18 ZIG ZAG

Paper foundation piecing allows even absolute beginners to achieve perfect points every time. A modern palette of lemon yellows and every shade of grey from smoke to dark ash make a quilt that's just right for a thoroughly modern baby.

For one block you will need
Finished block size:
4" x 6" (10.2 x 15.2cm)
- Two scraps of yellow prints, each 3" x 8" (7.6 x 20.3cm)
- Two scraps of grey prints/solids, each 3" x 8" (7.6 x 20.3cm)

Assembling the block
1. Download and print (see page 224 for link) or photocopy one copy of Zig Zag foundation A (page 225).
2. Following the general instructions for paper foundation piecing (page 21), piece the block in numerical order, trimming the seam allowances as you go. Leave the paper intact until all edges have been sewn to other blocks.

Modern quilts don't always need modern fabrics – look in your stash for assorted scraps. The design and colour palette will lend a modern look whatever fabrics are used.

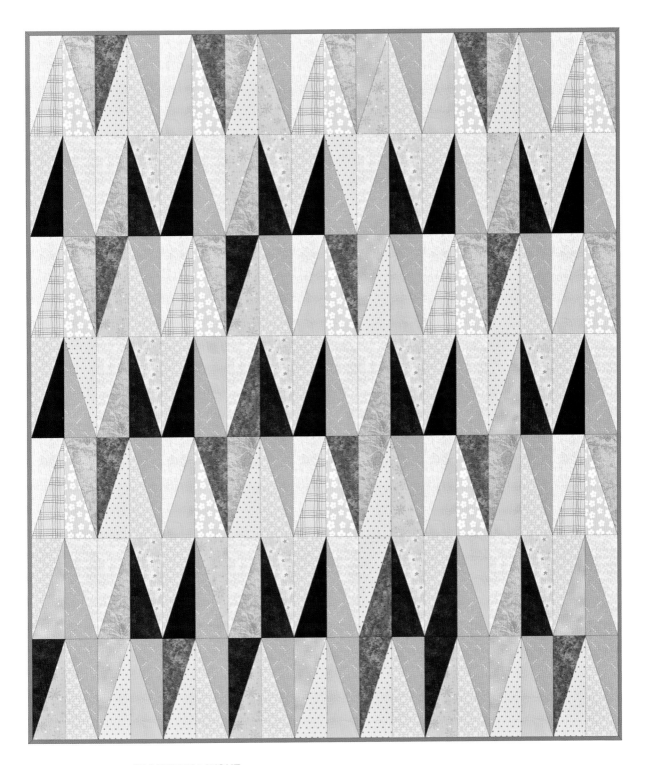

SUGGESTED LAYOUT

For my virtual quilt, which finishes at 36" x 42" (91.4 x 106.7cm), I created sixty-three blocks and sewed them together in seven rows of nine. Each alternate row switched the colour combinations, so odd rows had a yellow triangle on a grey background and even rows had a grey triangle on a yellow background. Bind the quilt with grey solid.

SPOOL OF THREAD

Sometimes it's hard to let go of the very last piece of a favourite print, but with my spools block you can preserve even the thinnest piece and enjoy it forever. Tuck this gorgeous little wall hanging into a corner of your sewing room as a permanent reminder of all your favourite scraps.

For one block you will need

Finished block size:
8" x 11" (20.3 x 28cm)

- Six to ten strips of co-ordinating prints, solids and tone on tone scraps
- 3" x 18" (7.6 x 45.7cm) piece of grey/brown for the spool
- Scraps for the block background

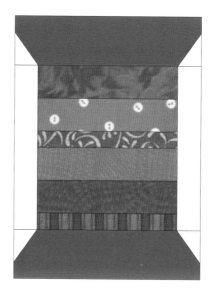

Assembling the block

1. Download and print (see page 224 for link) or photocopy one of each of Spool of Thread foundations A, B and C (page 227).

2. Following the general instructions for paper foundation piecing (page 21), piece the units in numerical order, trimming the seam allowances as you go.

SUGGESTED LAYOUT

For my virtual quilt I have made twelve spool blocks and sewn them together with 1" (2.5cm) finished sashing. The verticals match the background and the horizontals are in brown to give the look of wooden shelves. The final border is 1" (2.5cm) finished, too, giving a mini quilt that measures 30" x 51" (76.2 x 129.5cm).

20 ROMAN HOLIDAY

I take any opportunity I can to divide a block up into half light and half dark, Log Cabin style. It gives me so many possible arrangements of the finished blocks. Strip piecing the fabrics turns even the thinnest strips into something useable and my method makes two blocks for the work of one!

For two blocks you will need
Finished block size:
10" (25.4cm) square
- Approximately fourteen strips of bright scraps between 2" (5.1cm) and 15" (38.1cm) long and 1" (2.5cm) and 3" (7.6cm) wide
- One 10⅞" (26.7cm) square of cream tone on tone print

Assembling the block
1. Sew the strips of bright prints together as shown to make a panel approximately 12" (30.5cm) square.
2. Press the pieced panel carefully, then cut it into a 10⅞" (27.6cm) square, centring the centre diagonal strip as shown.
3. Lay the pieced and the plain squares right together, and mark the diagonal in pencil. Pin together carefully, then sew ¼" (6mm) either side of the pencil line.
4. Cut apart on the pencil line and press the two blocks.

Use a check or stripe for binding a quilt. It adds extra interest to a quilt with absolutely no extra work!

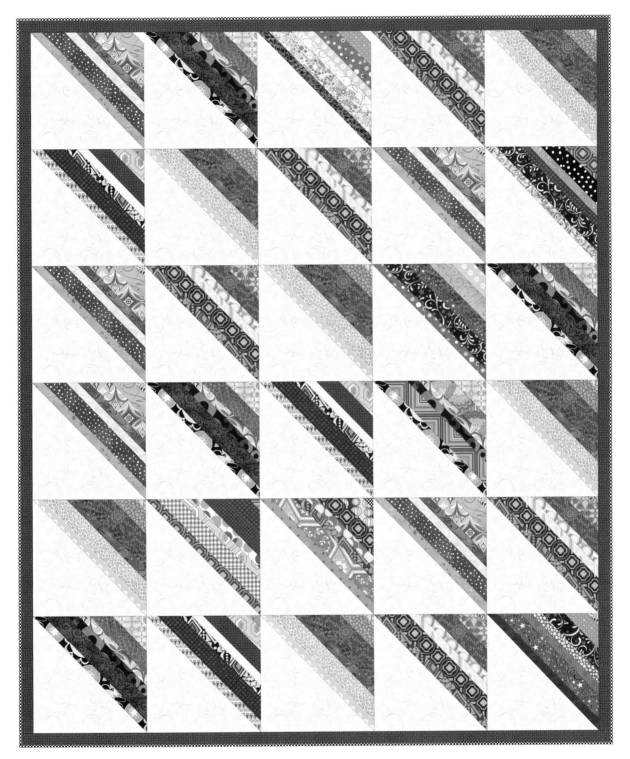

SUGGESTED LAYOUT

For my virtual quilt I made thirty blocks – that's just fifteen strip-pieced panels and fifteen squares of cream to make a quilt that is 52" x 62" (132 x 157.4cm). There's a 1" (2.5cm) finished border to contain the vibrant blocks and a final binding of black-and-white check.

UNION JACK

Patriotic and bang on trend, the Union Jack flag gets a scrappy makeover in my paper pieced quilt. Don't be alarmed by the idea of joining units together with regular piecing to make this block, it's a straightforward process. Be warned though, no one ever stops at one, these blocks are so addictive to make!

SUGGESTED LAYOUT

For my quilt I have set fifteen Union Jack blocks in three rows of five with 2" (5.1cm) finished sashing and 2" (5.1cm) square finished cornerstones using a traditional red, white and blue palette. Borders one and two finish at 1" (2.5cm) and border three at 4" (10.2cm) for an 80" x 94" (203.2 x 238.8cm) finished quilt. What a great college or university quilt this would make!

For one block you will need

Finished block size:
14"x 20" (35.6 x 50.8cm)
- Approximately 10" (25cm) white solid for the background stripes
- Scraps of three other solids for the crosses and background triangles

Assembling the block

1. Download and print (see page 224 for link) or photocopy two copies each of Union Jack foundations A and B (page 228).
2. Following the general instructions for paper foundation piecing (page 21), to piece the four units in numerical order, trimming the seam allowances as you go. Use one consistent colour for the centre diagonal stripe and cross, white for the stripes each side and a different solid for the triangles in each corner.
3. Trim the edges carefully, leaving a ¼" (6mm) seam allowance all around each unit.
4. From the third solid scrap cut two rectangles, each 2½" x 5½" (6.4 x 14cm), and one rectangle 2½" x 20½" (6.4 x 52cm).
5. Join a foundation A and a foundation B to either side of the 5½" (14cm) rectangle. Orientate the blocks with care! Make two.
6. Join the two rows made in step 5 to the 20½" (52cm) centre strip. Press the seams towards the wide centre cross. Leave the paper intact until all blocks have been sewn together.

WHIRLING GEESE

Two traditional blocks combine to make a quilt that looks so much more complex than it actually is. I've used a couple of different techniques in this quilt to make piecing as fast and accurate as possible. Familiarize yourself with the techniques before you start.

SUGGESTED LAYOUT

In my virtual quilt I have set twenty-five 54-40 or Fight blocks alternately with twenty-four Goose Chase blocks in seven rows of seven to create a quilt that is 86" x 86" (218.4 x 218.4cm), including a 1" (2.5cm) finished border. Remove the foundation papers once the border has been sewn on.

Pre-cut patches for foundation piecing approximately ½" (12mm) bigger on all sides. This makes piecing faster and helps to minimize waste.

For one 54-40 or Fight block you will need

Finished block size: 12" (30.5cm) square

- Eight 2½" (6.4cm) squares of cream/tan prints, for the four-patch units
- Eight 2½" (6.4cm) squares of brown prints, for the four-patch units
- One 4½" (11.4cm) square of brown print, for the four-patch units
- Four cream/tan print rectangles, each 3½" x 5½" (8.9 x 14cm) cut on one diagonal (yields eight triangles) for the foundation-pieced units
- Four 5" (12.7cm) squares of brown prints for the foundation-pieced units

Assembling the 54-40 or Fight block

1. Sew one brown and one cream/tan 2½" (6.4cm) square together. Make a total of eight units. Sew them in pairs to make four four-patch units.
2. Download and print (see page 224 for link) or photocopy four copies of Whirling Geese foundation A (page 225). Follow the general instructions (page 21) to foundation piece the four units.
3. Arrange the four-patch units, foundation-pieced units and centre square as shown. Sew the units together into rows.
4. Sew the rows together. Leave the paper intact until the blocks have all been sewn together.

For one Goose Chase block you will need

Finished block size: 12" (30.5cm) square

- Four squares of different brown prints, each 4⅞" (12.4cm) square, cut on one diagonal (yields eight triangles – four will be spare for another block)
- Four squares of different cream/tan prints, each 4⅞" (12.4cm) square, cut on one diagonal (yields eight triangles – four will be spare for another block)
- Two 5¼" (13.3cm) squares of brown print for the flying geese
- Eight 2⅞" (7.3cm) squares of cream and tan prints for the Flying Geese 'sky'
- One 3⅜" (8.6cm) square of brown print for the centre unit
- Two 3" (7.6cm) squares of cream/tan prints cut on one diagonal (yields four triangles) for the centre unit

Assembling the Goose Chase block

1. Make four half square triangle (HST) units with the 4⅞" (12.4cm) triangles.
2. Make two sets of Flying Geese using the no-waste method (eight Flying Geese units in total). See page 20.
3. Sew the four corner triangles to the centre brown square to make a square in a square unit.
4. Sew the units into rows and the rows together as shown.

23 JAPANESE LANTERN

If you can't resist those beautiful oriental prints and your stash is threatening to take over, make a batch of my Japanese Lantern blocks and create your very own display. The block is easily pieced with the stitch and flip technique (see page 20) – it's easy, fast and accurate!

For one block you will need

Finished block size: 9" (22.9cm) square

- Twelve 2" (5.1cm) squares of background fabric
- Two strips of medium oriental print each 9½" x 2" (24.1 x 5.1cm)
- Two strips of light oriental print each 9½" x 2" (24.1 x 5.1cm)
- Two strips of medium tone on tone for the lantern top and base, each 2" x 6½" (5.1 x 16.5cm)

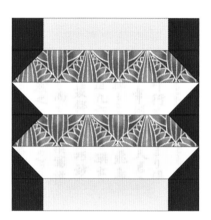

Assembling the block

1. Take eight of the background squares and mark the diagonal lightly in pencil. Pin a marked square to each end of each of the oriental 'lantern' fabrics, right sides together, both light and dark, checking that the orientation of the marked line matches the diagram. Sew on the line on each square.
2. Flip the background square back – it should match up with the corners of the lantern strip. Press, then fold back and trim the excess lantern and background fabric, leaving a ¼" (6mm) seam allowance.
3. Sew a background square to each end of the lantern base and top.
4. Sew the rows together.

Sew the tassels onto your quilt once the quilting and binding is completed. It's much easier this way and the tassels won't get in the way while you're quilting.

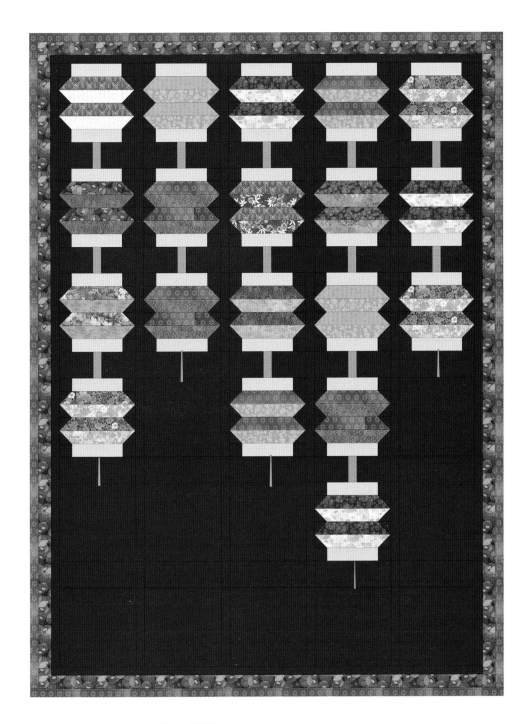

SUGGESTED LAYOUT

For my virtual quilt I've set nineteen lantern blocks with sashings – the vertical sashings are 1" (2.5cm) finished and the horizontal sashings are 3" (7.6cm) finished. Some of the horizontal sashings are pieced: the background strips finish at 4" x 3" (10.2 x 7.6cm) cut, and then there is a lantern connection, 1½" (3.8cm) cut to finish at 1" (2.5cm). I've added borders that finish at 1" (2.5cm), 1½" (3.8cm) and 1" (2.5cm). I've also added tassels to the ends of the lanterns for a really fun finish!

24 LATTICEWORK

I love Christmas and I can't resist making a new project or two each year for the holidays. There are always leftovers of Christmas fabrics and this beautiful quilt is a great way to use up the scraps. Use white or off-white for the latticework to really make your festive prints pop. This would also be a great quilt using oriental fabrics.

For one block you will need
Finished block size:
18" (45.7cm) square
- Approximately 10" (25cm) background fabric
- One 2½" x 26" (6.4 x 66cm) strip of Christmas fabric
- One 6½" (16.5cm) square of Christmas fabric
- Four 6" (15.2cm) squares of Christmas fabric cut on both diagonals (yields sixteen triangles)

Assembling the block
1. From the 2½" x 26" (6.4 x 66cm) strip of Christmas fabric, cut four rectangles each 2½" x 6½" (6.4 x 16.5cm).
2. From the background fabric cut eight rectangles, each 2½" x 6½" (6.4 x 16.5cm).
3. Sew one Christmas rectangle and two background rectangles together as shown to make the middle units.
4. Download and print (see page 224 for link) or photocopy four copies each of Latticework foundations A and B (page 228).
5. Following the general instructions for paper foundation piecing (page 21), piece the four corner units in numerical order from the remaining background fabric and Christmas triangles, trimming the seam allowances as you go.
6. Join the foundation-pieced units, the strip-pieced units and the centre square into rows, then join the rows. Leave the paper intact until all edges have been sewn to other blocks.

If you don't have enough themed fabrics you can always supplement what you have with batiks, prints and other feature fabrics from your scrap box. This also works if you don't have quite enough of one print to make a whole block.

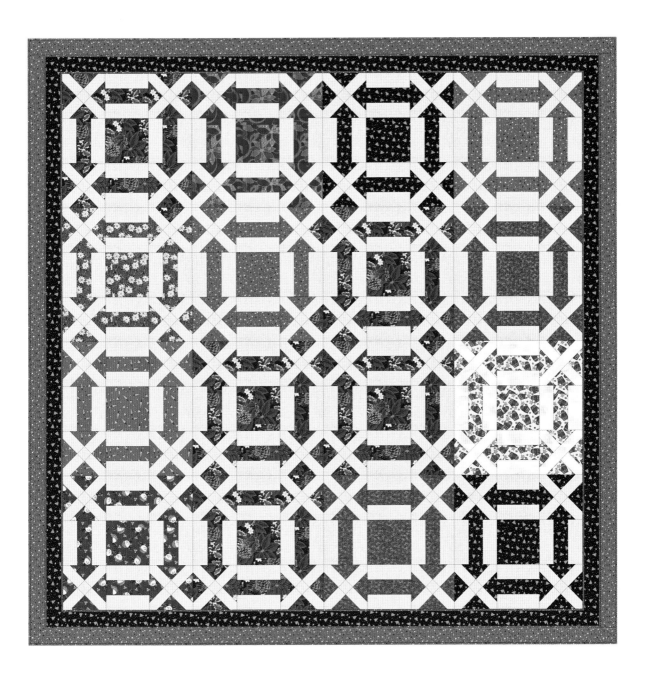

SUGGESTED LAYOUT

For my virtual quilt I have made sixteen Latticework blocks and set them together in four rows of four. I've added a narrow flange in red (see page 29) then a 2" (5.1cm) finished border in black Christmas print, another narrow flange and another 2" (5.1cm) finished border in Christmas green before binding in red. The quilt finishes at 80" x 80" (203.2 x 203.2cm) – wouldn't it make a perfect Christmas quilt for special visitors?

SCRAPS OF PEEL

The traditional Pickle Dish block gets a very classy scrap makeover and turns a bunch of unpromising odds and ends into a quilt to be admired. Foundation piecing is the perfect method for exceptional accuracy and the curves are not so hard to piece if you pin well and take your time!

For one block you will need

Finished block size: 9" (22.9cm) square

- Eighteen scraps of dark rust each approximately 2½" (6.4cm) square
- Sixteen scraps of assorted orange, yellow, gold and red prints, solids and tone on tones, each approximately 2½" (6.4cm) square
- One ellipse of dark rust print cut using template B Scraps of Peel (page 229)
- Two 2" (5.1cm) squares of pale orange for the corner squares
- Two triangles of dark golden yellow prints cut using template C Scraps of Peel (page 229)

Assembling the block

1. Download and print (see page 224 for link) or photocopy two copies of Scraps of Peel foundation A (page 229) and one copy each of templates B and C. Following the general instructions on page 21, foundation piece both foundation A arcs from the dark rust and assorted orange, yellow, gold and red prints, trimming the seam allowances as you go. Trim the paper to the ¼" (6mm) seam allowance all around.

2. Sew one arc to one edge of the centre ellipse (template B).

3. Sew a corner square to each end of the remaining foundation-pieced arc. Sew this arc to the other side of the ellipse.

4. Sew a golden yellow triangle (template C) to each side of the arcs.

5. Remove the foundation papers.

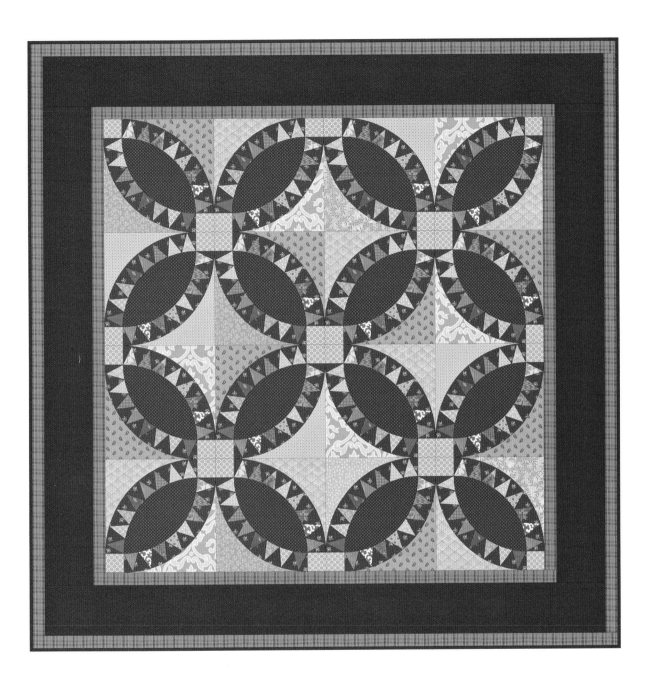

SUGGESTED LAYOUT

For my virtual quilt I made sixteen blocks and pieced them together in four rows of four. I added borders that finish at 1" (2.5cm), 4" (10.2cm) and finally 1" (2.5cm) to frame the blocks perfectly. The finished quilt is 48" x 48" (122 x122cm) – great for a wall quilt!

26 STRING SQUARES

Dynamic, modern and a true stash buster, no one needs to know that this is also as easy as A, B, C! Gather your collection of light and dark strips and start stitching. A 15½" (or larger) square ruler makes squaring up a piece of cake, too!

SUGGESTED LAYOUT

For my virtual quilt I set thirty-six blocks together and created interesting secondary patterns by turning some of the blocks. A design wall is helpful for this. The finished quilt measures 90" x 90" (228.6 x 228.6cm),

For one block you will need

Finished block size: 15" (38.1cm) square
- Lots of strips of fabric in various widths, from ½" (12mm) up to about 2" (5.1cm), in a good mix of lights and darks

Assembling the block

1. Start by sorting your fabrics into two piles – lights and darks.
2. Start with a short strip, about 2" (5.1cm) long. Sew a slightly longer strip beneath it. Keep adding strips in this way, alternating light and dark, until you reach the centre of what will be your finished square, then start to use shorter strips until you finish your square (which should be approximately 17" x 17"/43 x 43cm).
3. Trim the block to 15½" x 15½" (39.4 x 39.4cm), centring the middle diagonal.

TH!S WAY AND THAT!

Wedgwood blues, putty and pale cream make a quilt that is restful and calming. A wide variety of scraps can still have a cohesive look if the design is strong and you take care to place lights and darks in the correct position. A border of half square triangles adds a beautiful frame – and although I've shown it in one fabric, a variety of scraps would look even better!

SUGGESTED LAYOUT

My virtual quilt consists of sixty-four blocks followed by a 1½" (3.8cm) border then a border of half square triangles (HSTs), which finishes at 3" (7.6cm). You will need a total of 104 HST units. The final border finishes at 1½" (3.8cm). The finished quilt measures 84" x 84" (213.3 x 213.3cm),

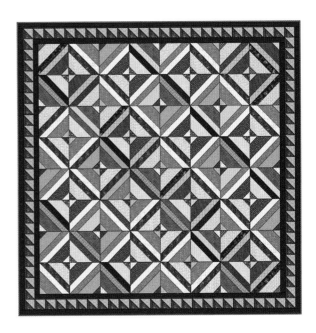

This block could be strip pieced and each block trimmed to 9½" x 9½" (24.1 x 24.1cm) on point; however, you wouldn't get the various strips to match so easily where the blocks join.

For one block you will need

Finished block size: 9" (22.9cm) square
- Three strips of various blues
- Three strips of various creams and putty prints

Assembling the block

1. Download and print (see page 224 for link) or photocopy one copy of This Way and That foundation A (page 229).
2. Following the general instructions on page 21, foundation piece the block in numerical order, trimming the seam allowances as you go. Leave the paper intact until all the blocks have been sewn together.

STRING STARS

This is my scrappy version of the traditional Lemoyne Star and I've made the star from string-pieced scraps. Many blocks can be given a string-pieced makeover, including house blocks, square in a square and basket blocks. Use one unifying background fabric or a mixture of scraps, it's up to you. Paper foundation piecing makes for a very accurate block with perfect points and no set-in seams.

For one block you will need

Finished block size:

15" (38.1cm) square

- Thin strips of a wide variety of light print fabrics
- One dark scrap fabric for the background

Assembling the block

1. Sew the thin strips together to make a piece of fabric that is at least 9" x 5" (22.9 x 12.7cm). Any width of strip/scrap can be used, but I recommend that they are no thinner than 1" (2.5cm) and no wider than 3" (7.6cm).

2. Download and print (see page 224 for link) or photocopy four copies each of String Stars foundations A and B (see page 230).

3. Following the general instructions on page 21, foundation piece the units in numerical order, using the string-pieced fabric piece to cover number 1 on both foundation A and B, and trimming seam allowances as you go. Use a unifying background fabric for pieces 2 and 3.

4. When you have foundation pieced all eight of the foundations, trim them, leaving your ¼" (6mm) seam allowance, then join A and B foundations in pairs.

5. Join the pairs into rows and finally join the rows to make one string-pieced Lemoyne Star block. Leave the paper intact until all the blocks have been sewn together.

SUGGESTED LAYOUT

For my virtual quilt I made sixteen String Star blocks, eight with light stars and dark backgrounds and eight with dark stars and light backgrounds. The star blocks are joined with 2″ (5.1cm) wide finished sashing and 2″ (5.1cm) finished cornerstones. I then added a 5″ (12.7cm) finished border. My finished quilt measures 80″ (203.3cm) square.

COVENT GARDEN

Inspiration for a block or quilt can come at any time, and this quilt is a prime example. I was halfway to where I wanted to get to on the London Underground and as we stopped at Covent Garden I saw a design in the wall tiles. It was enough to make me get off the train to take photographs and the result was this handsome and rather masculine quilt.

SUGGESTED LAYOUT

For my quilt I have pieced forty Covent Garden blocks and sewn them in a 5 x 8 arrangement. This makes a quilt that is 80" x 88" (203.2 x 223.5cm).

For one block you will need

Finished block size: 11" x 16" (28 x 40.7cm)

- 1½" (3.8cm) strips of assorted medium/dark prints, approximately 10" (25cm) in total
- 1½" (3.8cm) strips of assorted grey/white prints, approximately 10" (25cm) in total, for the background

To speed up the construction, you could strip piece some or all of the rows. For example, to strip piece row 6 cut 4½" (11.4cm) wide strips (approximately 16" or 40cm long) of two medium/dark prints and two grey prints. Sew together medium/dark + grey + medium/dark + grey. Press the seams towards the medium/dark prints. Subcut 1½" (3.8cm) strips from the unit. You should get approximately ten strips from one strip.

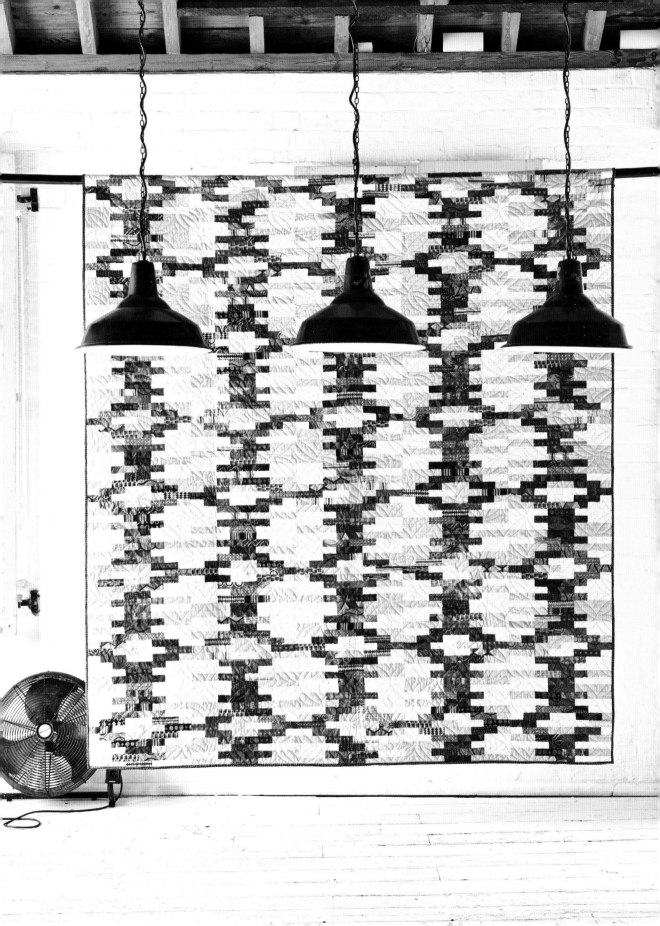

COVENT GARDEN

Assembling the block

1. The block is made up of eleven rows but there are actually only four repeated rows. Rows 1, 3, 9 and 11 are made by joining a 1½" x 6½" (3.8 x 16.5cm) strip in grey, a 1½" x 4½" (3.8 x 11.4cm) strip in medium/dark print and a 1½" x 6½" (3.8 x 16.5cm) strip in grey.

2. Rows 2, 4, 8 and 10 are made by joining a 1½" x 4½" (3.8 x 11.4cm) strip in grey, a 1½" x 4½" (3.8 x 11.4cm) strip in medium/dark print, a 1½" x 4½" (3.8 x 11.4cm) strip in medium/dark print and a 1½" x 4½" (3.8 x 11.4cm) strip in grey.

3. Rows 5 and 7 are made by joining a 1½" x 2½" (3.8 x 6.4cm) strip in grey, a 1½" x 4½" (3.8 x 11.4cm) strip in medium/dark print, a 1½" x 4½" (3.8 x 11.4cm) strip in grey, a 1½" x 4½" (3.8 x 11.4cm) strip in medium/dark print and a 1½" x 2½" (3.8 x 6.4cm) strip in grey.

4. Row 6 is made by joining a 1½" x 4½" (3.8 x 11.4cm) strip in medium/dark print, a 1½" x 4½" (3.8 x 11.4cm) strip in grey, a 1½" x 4½" (3.8 x 11.4cm) strip in grey and a 1½" x 4½" (3.8 x 11.4cm) strip in medium/dark prints.

5. Sew the rectangles together to make each row and press your seam allowances towards the medium/dark prints. Use an accurate ¼" (6mm) seam throughout.

6. Sew the eleven rows together in order. Centre each row on the previous row. Press the seams open to reduce bulk. Trim the finished block to 11½" x 16½" (29.2 x 42cm).

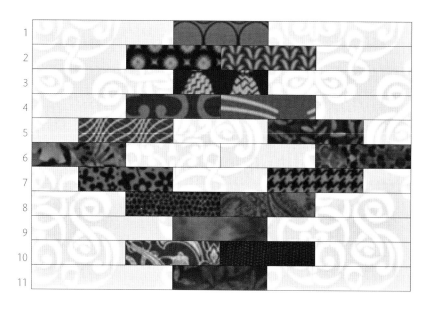

30 SPIDER'S WEB

This quilt looks great in your favourite colour family – or you can throw everything you have at it! The secret is to make sure that there is a good contrast between the spider's web fabrics and the stars. Here I've used up black-and-white print scraps and every yellow, green and lime solid scrap I could find!

SUGGESTED LAYOUT

In my virtual quilt I have pieced together twenty-five spider's web blocks in five rows of five for a quilt that finishes at 35" x 35" (89 x 89cm), a great size for a table topper or small wall quilt. Add a further two rows for a sweet baby quilt that measures 35" x 49" (89 x 124.5cm).

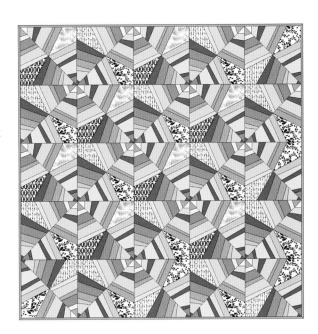

Press your blocks without steam as you are making them. Steam can distort or shrink your paper foundation. Once the papers have been removed you can press with steam if you wish.

For one block you will need

Finished block size: 7" (17.8cm) square

- Two large black-and-white scraps, each approximately 4" x 6" (10 x 15cm)
- Approximately twenty-four scraps of assorted lime, green and yellow solids in various widths from ½" (12mm) up to 2" (5.1cm)

Assembling the block

1. Download and print (see page 224 for link) or photocopy Spider's Web foundations A and B (page 230).
2. Following the general instructions on page 21, foundation piece the two units in numerical order, trimming the seam allowances as you go.
3. Sew the units together. Leave the paper intact until all the blocks have been sewn together.

31 STRIPS AND SNOWBALLS

Easy strip piecing and stitch and flip corners (see page 20) make this quilt super easy, super fast and a super way to use up lots of scrap strips quickly.

For one block you will need

Finished block size:
10" (25.4cm) square

- Eight–ten strips of black-and-white prints between 1" (2.5cm) and 3" (7.6cm) in width and all at least 10½" (26.7cm) long
- Two 2½" (6.4cm) squares of dark grey solid
- Two 2½" (6.4cm) squares of light grey solid

Assembling the block

1. Sew the various strips of black-and-white prints together to form a panel at least 10½" x 10½" (26.7 x 26.7cm).
2. Trim the pieced panel to exactly 10½" x 10½" (26.7 x 26.7cm).
3. On the back of the four solid squares, draw one diagonal lightly in pencil.
4. Pin the squares to the four corners of the pieced block, right sides together, making sure that the drawn diagonal line goes from one side of the block to the adjacent side. Note that the light grey squares are in diagonally opposite corners, as are the dark grey solid squares.
5. Sew along the drawn line, making sure that your stitched line cuts across the corners.
6. Press the solid corners back, then trim the excess from underneath, leaving a ¼" (6mm) seam allowance.

If you do not always have a full 10½" (26.7cm) strip of the same print for a block, just piece two or more strips together to get the required length. It is patchwork, after all!

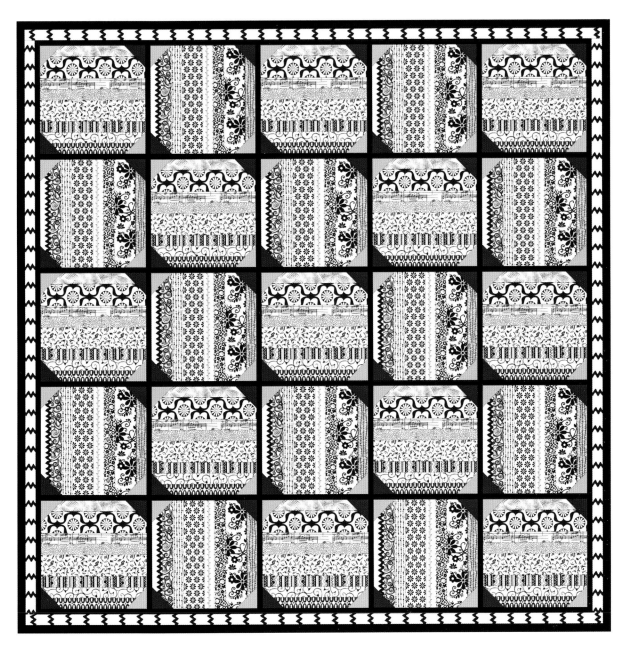

SUGGESTED LAYOUT

My virtual quilt sets twenty-five blocks in five rows of five, with ½" (12mm) finished sashing and a ½" (12mm), 1" (2.5cm) and final ½" (12mm) finished border. My finished quilt is 56" x 56" (142 x 142cm).

TRIPLE CROSS

I love scrap quilts where you throw just about everything into the mix and keep your fingers crossed! A uniform background fabric and a good, strong sashing will help to contain the scraps. Try not to judge the individual blocks as you make them: with scrap quilting, the whole is often worth more than the sum of its parts!

For one block you will need

Finished block size:

10" (25.4cm) square

- Four 4½" (11.4cm) squares of print scrap 1
- Eight 2½" (6.4cm) squares of light background print
- Four 2½" (6.4cm) squares of print scrap 2
- Four 2½" (6.4cm) squares of print scrap 3
- Five 2½" (6.4cm) squares of print scrap 4

Assembling the block

1. Make the corner units first by using the stitch and flip method (page 20) to sew the light background squares and the print scrap 2 squares to three of the corners of print scrap square 1, as shown.
2. Sew the print scrap 3 and 4 squares together in pairs; you will have one print 4 left for the centre.
3. Sew the units together in rows, then sew the rows together to complete the block.

I always make more blocks than I'm going to need for a quilt. Blocks that refuse to play nicely with the others don't make it into the final quilt, but I do still use them. After layering them with batting (wadding) and backing, I can practise my quilting to see that it works with the design. They make great pillows and cushions, too.

SUGGESTED LAYOUT

For my virtual quilt I set thirty-six blocks together in six rows of six, joined with 1" (2.5cm) finished sashing, 1" (2.5cm) finished cornerstones and four borders that finish at 3½" (8.9cm), 1" (2.5cm), 1" (2.5cm) and 1" (2.5cm). My finished quilt measures 80" (203.2cm) square.

33 STRIPPY WATERWHEEL

Piecing your scraps together to make a larger piece of fabric is a brilliant way to use what you have to make what you want. It also adds far more visual interest to a quilt than a single fabric could ever offer. It's one of the beauties of scrap quilting and the thing that keeps me coming back again and again.

For two blocks you will need

Finished block size: 9" (22.9cm) square

- Eight–ten different light strips of fabric ½"–2" (1.2–5.1cm) wide and 10" (25.4cm) long
- Eight–ten different dark strips of fabric ½"–2" (1.2 –5.1cm) wide and 10" (25.4cm) long

Assembling the block

1. Sew all of the light strips together to make a panel approximately 10" x 10" (25.4 x 25.4cm). Press the seams one way.
2. Sew all of the dark strips together to make a panel approximately 10" x 10" (25.4 x 25.4cm) and once again, press the seams one way.
3. Use Strippy Waterwheel templates A and B (page 231) to cut one of each shape from each pieced panel. Change the direction of the pieced 'stripes' when you cut the lights and the darks. You should end up with a total of two As and two Bs.
4. Switch the colours around and re-sew the blocks.

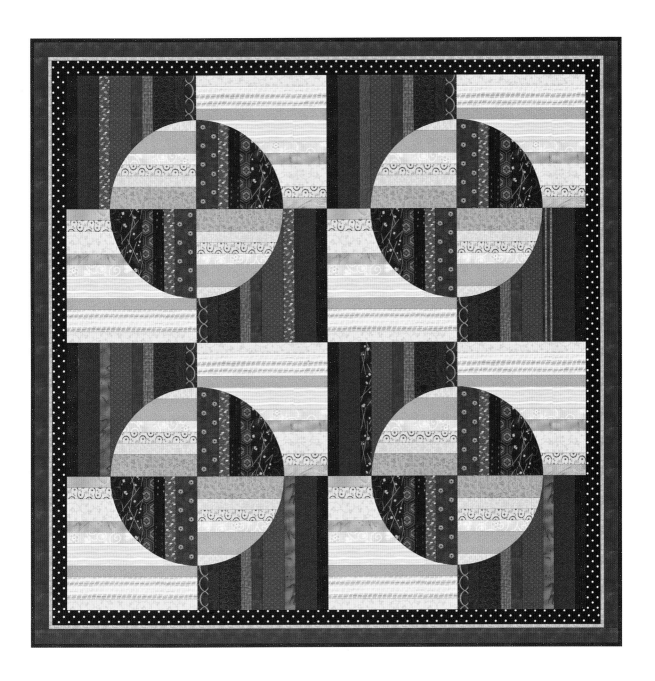

SUGGESTED LAYOUT

For my virtual quilt I used a total of sixteen blocks (pieced from eight light panels and eight dark panels), using a collection of tans mixed with browns, red ochre and deep rust. I added two outer borders that both finish at 1" (2.5cm) with a ¼" (6mm) folded flange border sandwiched between them (see page 27). The quilt is 40" x 40" (101.6 x 101.6cm).

34 TILTED

Inspired by a pile of books sitting on my desk, Tilted is an easy, modern quilt block and such a fun one to make! Don't follow my pattern slavishly: use whatever size strips you have, sew them together then simply trim to size at the end.

For one block you will need
Finished block size:
18" (45.7cm) square
- Six print scraps cut into rectangles, each 2½" (6.4cm) wide and 5½"–11½" (14 x 29.2cm) long
- Six print scraps cut into rectangles, each 1½" (3.8cm) wide and 5½"–12½" long (14 x 31.7cm)
- Background fabric cut into strips 1½" (3.8cm) and 2½" (6.4cm)

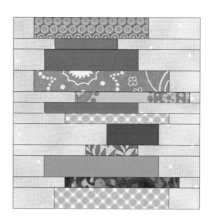

Assembling the block
1. Sew the background strips to each side of each of the print rectangles. Press the seam allowances towards the print rectangles.
2. Sew the rows together, allowing the 'pile' to tilt this way and that. Press the seams one way.
3. Trim the block to 18½" x 18½" (47 x 47cm). Keep the trimmed background strips for your next block!

A design wall makes placing your blocks much easier, as you can stand back and see how everything works together.
A piece of flannel pinned to the wall makes a very good stand-in!

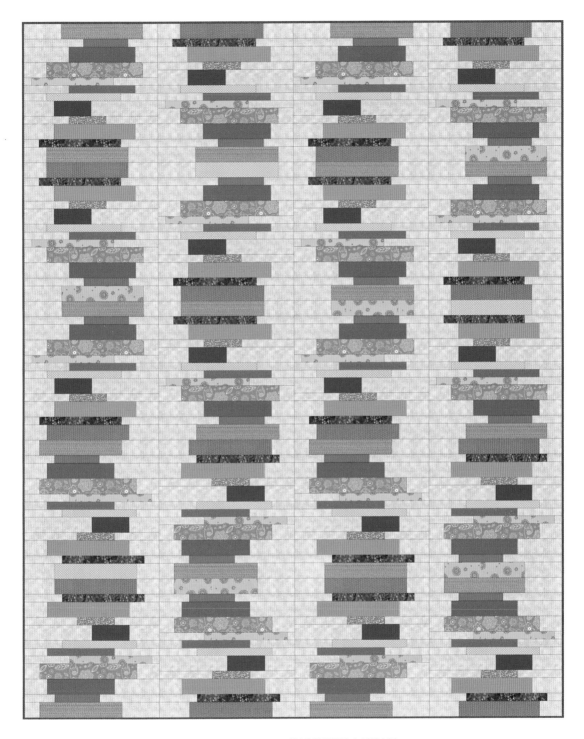

SUGGESTED LAYOUT

For my virtual quilt I made twenty blocks and set them together without sashing in a 4 x 5 arrangement. There's no border on this one: just quilt it and bind it, and you're done! The finished quilt is 72" x 90" (182.8 x 228.6cm).

35 ORANGE PEEL

A striking modern quilt that repackages a very traditional block. Often done in just two fabrics my interpretation makes it a modern scrap classic. A dark grey solid background helps to unify and showcase a collection of bright orange and gold scraps.

SUGGESTED LAYOUT

For my quilt I made a total of sixty-four blocks and set them edge to edge in eight rows of eight. I've added a 1" (2.5cm) finished border in dark grey and a binding in the same fabric. The quilt finishes at 82" x 82" (208.3 x 208.3cm).

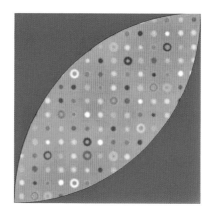

For one block you will need

Finished block size: 10" (25.4cm) square
- One 10½" (26.7cm) square of dark grey Essex linen
- One 10½" (26.7cm) square of assorted bright orange/gold print fabric

Assembling the block

1. Using the Orange Peel appliqué template (page 231), mark then cut one shape from orange fabric, adding a ¼" (6mm) turn-under allowance by eye.
2. Using either the starch and press or 'soft edge' turned appliqué method (see pages 25 and 26) prepare your shape for appliqué.
3. Pin the prepared appliqué to the background square, ensuring that you have left ¼" (6mm) allowance at the corners.
4. Sew the appliqué in place by hand with an appliqué stitch or by machine using a zig zag or blanket stitch

To stitch the appliqué edges faster, sew a row of eight background blocks together, pin the orange peel segments on, then appliqué one side of each, moving from one block to the next. At the end of the row, turn your work and appliqué the other edge in one continuous line of stitching.

SCRAP FRAME

Simple, classic blocks and patchwork frames build to make a stunning but surprisingly easy quilt. When piecing patchwork borders or frames it's essential to be accurate, so test your ¼" (6mm) seam before you start sewing the whole thing (see page 16)! These blocks are a whopping 36" (91.4cm) square, but you only need to make four to create this stunning quilt.

For one block you will need

Finished block size:

36" (91.4cm) square

- Scraps of various plum/purple prints and batiks
- Scraps of various gold, tan and cream prints, solids and batiks
- Scraps of various turquoise prints, solids and batiks

Assembling the block

1. Make the centre star from one 8½" (21.6cm) centre square, four Flying Geese units each 4½" x 8½" (11.4 x 21.6cm) and four corner squares each 4½" x 4½" (11.4 x 11.4cm). The Flying Geese units are make using the no-waste method, using a 9¼" (23.5cm) square of cream fabric and four 4⅞" (12.4cm) squares of various plum prints (see page 20).

2. Frame number one: four 2½" x 2½" (6.4 x 6.4cm) cornerstones in gold and four rectangles, each 2½" x 16½" (6.4 x 42cm), in various plum/gold prints.

3. Frame number two: forty-eight Flying Geese units each 2½" x 4½" (6.4 x 11.4cm). The Flying Geese units are made using the no-waste method using one 5¼" (13.3cm) square of turquoise print and four 2⅞" (7.3cm) squares of various creams. This makes four Flying Geese units at a time.

4. Frame number three: sixty 2½" (6.4cm) squares in various tans/creams.

5. Frame number four: four 2½" x 2½" (6.4 x 6.4cm) cornerstones in gold and four rectangles, each 2½" x 32½" (6.4x 82.5cm), in various plum/gold prints.

SUGGESTED LAYOUT

For my virtual quilt I sewed four Scrap Frame blocks together with 2" (5.1cm) finished sashing and 2" (5.1cm) finished cornerstones. I added a border of Flying Geese which each finish at 2" x 4" (5.1 x 10.2cm), the same size as in the frame block, and 4" (10.2cm) cornerstones. A final 2" (5.1cm) finished border frames the quilt and brings it up to 90" x 90" (228.6 x 228.6cm).

37 WONKY BOXES

Gather together your brightest scraps and piece this fun and dynamic scrap quilt. I've used a solid in the centre, but this would also be a great place to showcase a fussy-cut motif or some machine embroidery. My blocks are paper pieced for accuracy without any difficult measuring or cutting!

SUGGESTED LAYOUT

For my virtual quilt I set thirteen Wonky Boxes blocks on point, with side and corner setting triangles. For the large setting triangles cut a sheet of paper into a 14" (35.6cm) square, then cut on both diagonals to yield four triangles. Use one of the triangles as a template to cut eight side setting triangles. The corner triangles are a 7⅜" (18.7cm) square cut once on the diagonal. I've added a ¼" (6mm) finished flange border in orange (see page 27) and a 1" (2.5cm) finished border in a black-and-white stripe. The final ¼" (6mm) binding is in the same orange solid as the flange for a pop of colour. The finished quilt is approximately 41" x 41" (104 x 104cm).

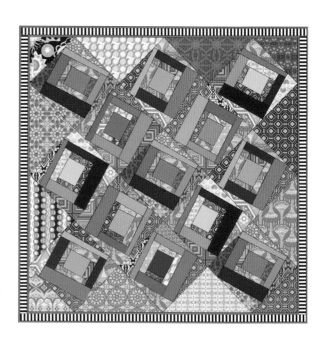

For one block you will need

Finished block size: 9" (22.9cm) square
- Eight bright print scraps at least 2" x 10" (5.1 x 25.4cm)
- Four bright solid scraps at least 2" x 8" (5.1 x 20.3cm)
- One bright solid scrap approximately 4" (10.2cm) square for the centre

Assembling the block

1. Download and print (see page 224 for link) or photocopy one copy of Wonky Boxes foundation A (page 232).
2. Following the general instructions on page 21, foundation piece the block in numerical order, trimming seam allowances as you go.
3. Trim the block to 9½" x 9½" (24.1 x 24.1cm). Leave the paper intact until all the blocks have been sewn together.

Foundation-pieced blocks are easy to enlarge or reduce on a photocopier to make the quilt larger or smaller.

38 HUNTER'S STAR

Hunter's Star is a fabulous traditional block, which usually gets a two-fabric treatment, most often turkey red and white. Here I've given a nod to the original with a strong red-and-white pinwheel but the rest of the quilt goes scrappy with a collection of indigo blues, ochres, golds and adder red.

SUGGESTED LAYOUT

For my virtual quilt I have pieced together thirty-six Hunter's Star blocks in six rows of six. I have then added a border of 4" (10.2cm) finished squares and 4" (10.2cm) finished half square triangle units (HSTs). To make the HST units, cut one square of red and one square of white/blue print at 4⅞" (12.4cm), and follow the general instructions on page 19. (You will need twenty-eight HSTs, made from fourteen squares of each fabric.)
The final border is 4" (10.2cm) finished and the whole quilt measures 88" x 88" (223.5 x 223.5cm).

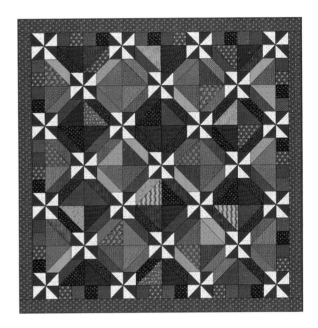

For one block you will need
Finished block size: 12" (30.5cm) square
- Two scraps of adder red/gold or brown
- Two scraps of indigo blue
- One solid red scrap cut to 5½" (14cm) square, then cut once on the diagonal (yields two triangles)
- One white/blue print scrap cut to 5½" (14cm) square, then cut once on the diagonal (yields two triangles)

Assembling the block

1. Download and print (see page 224 for link) or photocopy two copies of Hunter's Star foundation A (page 233).
2. Following the general instructions on page 21, foundation piece both units in numerical order, trimming seam allowances as you go. Note that the position of the red and white/blue print is reversed in each section.
3. Sew both foundations together and trim the block to 12½" (31.7cm) square. Leave the paper intact until all the blocks have been sewn together.

BULLSEYE

These psychedelic bullseyes are sure to grab attention wherever you choose to show off this quilt. Easy fusible appliqué make this project fast and achievable. It's a fabulous quilt for a teenager or as a striking piece of wall art and a great way to bust your stash of solids or batiks.

For one block you will need

Finished block size:
20" (50.8cm) square

- One 20½" (52cm) square of background fabric
- Four assorted scraps of various solids for the circle appliqués, approximately 18½" (47cm), 17" (43cm), 10" (25cm) and 6" (15cm) squares
- Fusible web

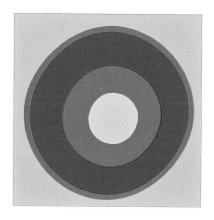

Assembling the block

1. Create four circular paper appliqué templates using a pair of compasses or by drawing around a plate or cup, with diameters approximately as follows: 18" (45.7cm), 16½" (42cm), 10" (25.4cm) and 5" (12.7cm).

2. Trace the largest circle appliqué template onto the paper side of the fusible web, then cut out the circle about ¼" (6mm) inside the drawn line. Roughly cut around the outside of the circle, cutting about ¼" (6mm) outside of the fusible web.

3. Iron the ring of fusible web to the back of your largest (18½"/47cm) square of appliqué fabric. Cut the circle out neatly on the drawn line, then peel the paper away. Fuse to the right side of your background square, placing the circle vaguely centrally. (This block is meant to be a little wonky!)

4. Repeat the first two steps using the cut-out fusible web circle and the second largest (17"/43cm) scrap square. Each time you should cut the centre of the paper away, leaving only a ring of fusible web. This keeps the appliqués soft and makes your fusible web go further!

5. Repeat for the third and fourth circles, fusing each one in place.

6. Sew around the edges of the circles using a small zig zag or blanket stitch. Use a toning or a wildly clashing colour! It's up to you!

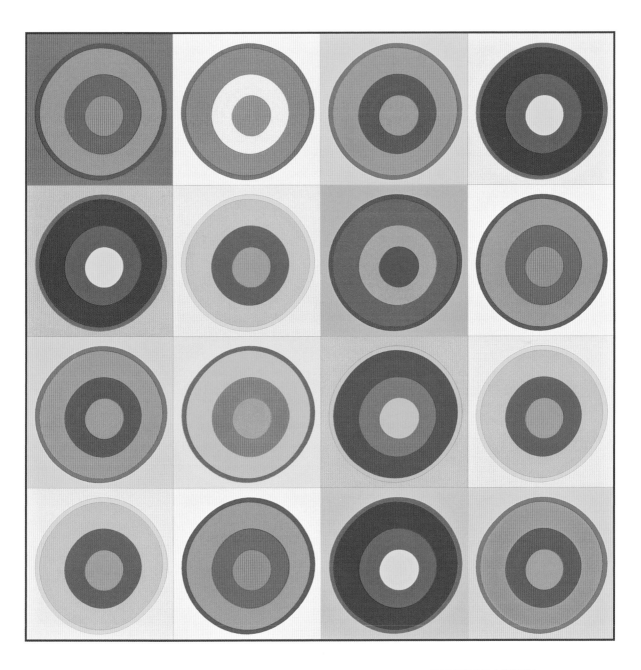

For my virtual quilt I set sixteen bullseye blocks together, edge to edge. This makes a quilt that is 80" x 80" (203.2 x 203.2cm).

Cover your appliqués with a sheet of non-stick baking parchment when you are fusing the circles to project your iron from the glue.

MAGIC CARPET

Richly hued and using every bright scrap you can find, bring order to chaos by placing your scraps carefully to create diagonal lines of colour. The real magic comes when you place the blocks together and see your design come to life. This block really will breathe magic into your scrap box!

SUGGESTED LAYOUT

For my virtual quilt I have arranged sixteen blocks together in four rows of four then added a ¼" (6mm) finished flange border in orange (see page 27), a border in blue damask print that finishes at 4" (10.2cm) and a final bright orange binding for a quilt that finishes at 65" x 65" (165.1 x 165.1cm).

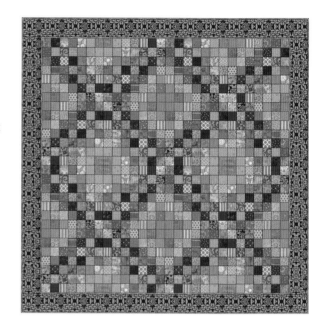

Use more colours in your quilt and create thirteen diagonal rows of different colours in each block. Keep these rows fairly (but not perfectly) consistent throughout the sixteen blocks and set them together. Magical!

For one block you will need

Finished block size: 14" (35.6cm) square

- Thirteen 2½" (6.4cm) squares of bright pink/magenta
- Twelve 2½" (6.4cm) squares of bright orange
- Twelve 2½" (6.4cm) squares of lime/bright green
- Twelve 2½" (6.4cm) squares of cobalt blue

Assembling the block

1. Sew the squares into vertical rows. Press the seams up on the odd-numbered rows and down on the even-numbered rows.
2. Sew the rows together.

DITSY SQUARES

This quilt would make a great project for using up a collection of charm squares and oddments of jelly rolls and strips. The piecing is simple and the only decision required is, light or dark pile? It's that easy!

SUGGESTED LAYOUT

For my virtual quilt I have set together twenty-five blocks in five rows of five to make a quilt centre that is 60½" (153.7cm) square. I've then added border number 1, which finishes at 1" (2.5cm), and border number 2, which finishes at 3½" (8.9cm), making a quilt that is 69" x 69" (175.2 x 175.2cm).

For one block you will need

Finished block size: 12" (30.5cm) square

- Six 2⅞" (7.3cm) squares of light/pastel, each cut once on the diagonal (yields twelve triangles)
- Six 2⅞" (7.3cm) dark squares, cut once on the diagonal (yields twelve triangles)
- Twelve 2½" (6.4cm) squares of light/pastel
- Twelve 2½" (6.4cm) dark squares

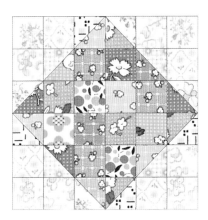

Assembling the block

1. Start by making a total of twelve half square triangle (HST) units by sewing the light and dark triangles together. Press the seam allowances towards the dark fabric.
2. Arrange the light/pastel squares, the HST units and the dark squares to create the block.
3. Sew the units together into six rows, then sew the rows together.

POSITIVE
AND NEGATIVE

A really fun block that makes use of both the positive and negative spaces. Pair one bright novelty print scrap with white solid and make two blocks for the price of one!

For two blocks you will need
Finished block size:
6" x 5" (15.2 x 12.7cm)
- One rectangle of bright print, approximately 8" x 6" (20 x 15cm)
- One rectangle of white solid, approximately 8" x 6" (20 x 15cm)

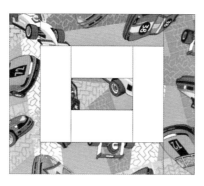

Assembling the block

1. Place the fabrics right sides together and cut the following: two rectangles each 1½" x 5½" (3.8 x 14cm), two rectangles each 4½" x 1½" (11.4 x 3.8cm), two rectangles each 3½" x 1½" (8.9 x 3.8cm) and three rectangles each 1½" x 2½" (3.8 x 6.4cm). As you are cutting two layers of fabric, you will have double this number of pieces (eighteen in total).

2. Rearrange the cut pieces to make the two blocks as shown: one positive, one negative.

3. Sew the pieces together as shown. Press the seams towards the darker fabric where possible.

Use a variety of conversational and novelty prints for a quilt that is both fun and educational. Play 'I spy' and 'Can you find...?' games with your toddler.

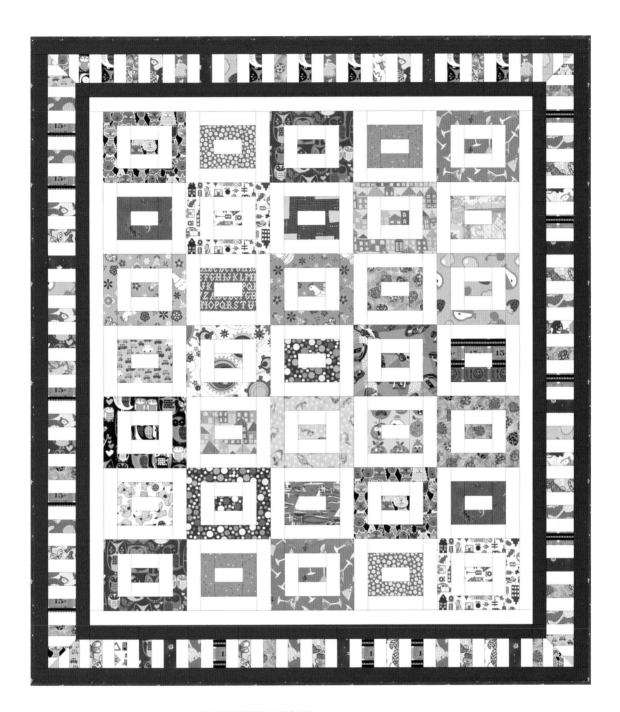

SUGGESTED LAYOUT

For my virtual quilt I have pieced a total of thirty-five blocks (eighteen sets of fabrics, one block is spare) and sewn them together in a seven rows of five. Borders 1 and 3 finish at 1" (2.5cm) and the second border is made up of 1½" (3.8cm) wide strips of print fabrics sewn together with 1½" (3.8cm) strips of white solid. This piano-key border finishes at 3" (7.6cm) wide for a finished quilt that measures 40" x 45" (101.6 x 114.3cm) – perfect for a toddler quilt.

43 BOURGOYNE SURROUNDED

I took a very traditional patchwork block and supersized it, which is a great thing to do if your scraps are fairly large and abundant but your time is not. Nine blocks and some sashing and the quilt is made – and at a whopping 110" x 110" (279.4 x 279.4cm), this quilt will fit a king-sized bed with ease. I have followed a modern approach to scrap quilting here and used many scraps, but in a narrowly defined colourway of gold, tan and red. It's classic with a scrap twist.

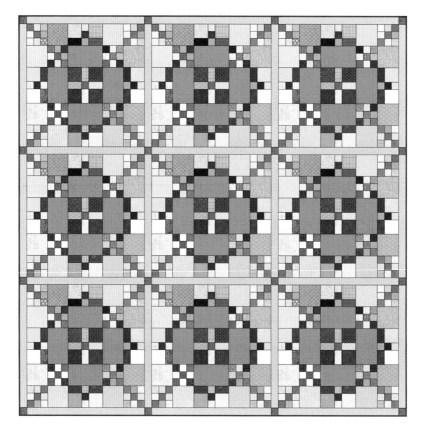

SUGGESTED LAYOUT

For my quilt I made nine Burgoyne Surrounded blocks and joined them together in three rows of three with twenty-four 2" x 34" (5.1cm x 86.4cm) sashing pieces in various cream/tan prints and sixteen 2" (5.1cm) square cornerstones in various red prints. The finished quilt is 110" x 110" (279.4 x 279.4cm) and is bound in a tan print.

BOURGOYNE SURROUNDED

43

For one block you will need

Finished block size:

34" (86.4cm) square

- Forty-eight assorted tan/cream 2½"
  (6.4cm) squares
- Thirty-seven assorted red 2½"
  (6.4cm) squares
- Eight assorted tan/cream 6½"
  (16.5cm) squares
- Eight assorted red 2½" x 4½" (6.4 x
  11.4cm) rectangles
- Eight assorted tan/cream 4½"
  (11.4cm) squares
- Four gold 6½" x 10½" (16.5 x 26.7cm)
  rectangles
- Four assorted 2½" x 4½" (6.4 x
  11.4cm) tan/cream rectangles
- Four assorted red 4½" (11.4cm)
  squares

middle unit

Assembling the block

1. Using six cream/tan and three red 2½" (6.4cm) squares, make up unit 1.
   Make a total of four units.
2. Using five red and four cream/tan 2½" (6.4cm) squares, make up unit 2.
   Make a total of four units
3. Sew the unit 1 and unit 2s to the 6½" (16.5cm) tan/cream squares to make
   the corner units. Make four in total. Set aside.
4. Sew one 2½" x 4½" (6.4 x 11.4cm) red rectangle to a 4½" (11.4cm) tan/cream
   square to make unit 3. Make eight in total.
5. Sew one cream/tan 2½" (6.4cm) square to opposite sides of a 2½" (6.4cm)
   red square, to make unit 4. Make four in total.
6. Sew one unit 3 to each side of a unit 4, then sew this unit to one long side of
   a gold 6½" x 10½" x (16.5 x 26.7cm) rectangle to make the middle units. Make
   four in total. Set aside.
7. Sew a 4½" (11.4cm) red square to opposite long sides of a cream/tan 2½" x 4½"
   (6.4 x 11.4cm) rectangle. Make two, then sew the remaining two cream/tan
   2½" x 4½" (6.4 x 11.4cm) rectangles to opposite
   sides of the last red 2½" (6.4cm) square. Sew these three rows together to
   make the block centre.
8. Finally sew the units together into rows and then join the rows to make
   the block.

SIMPLE TILES

A simple change to a classic block creates a new modern look. Dig out your bright scraps and team with a multi-coloured pin dot to tie all the crazy colours together.

SUGGESTED LAYOUT

My virtual quilt contains a total of thirty-five blocks in five rows of seven. There are eighteen blocks as described in the instructions and seventeen alternate blocks. This quilt finishes at 63" x 75" (160 x 190.5cm).

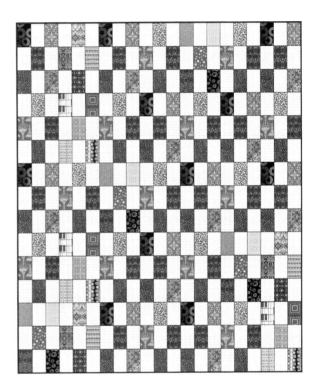

I like to make sure that the blocks in the corners of a scrap quilt have good strong colours in them to help 'anchor' the quilt and provide a pleasing edge.

For one block you will need

Finished block size: 9" x 15" (22.9 x 38.1cm)

- Four bright scraps cut to 3½" x 5½" (8.9 x 14cm)
- Five white/multi pin-dot rectangles, each 3½" x 5½" (8.9 x 14cm)

Assembling the block

1. Lay the nine rectangles out as shown and sew together in rows. Press the seam allowances towards the bright rectangles.
2. Sew the rows together.
3. The alternate block contains four white/multi pin-dot rectangles and five bright scraps.

DRESDEN SUNFLOWERS

I can't look at sunflowers without smiling and I feel the same way about this quilt. Don't be put off by those curved edges: yes, they are appliquéd, but using lightweight interfacing. It's a fun and easy method, – you're going to love it!

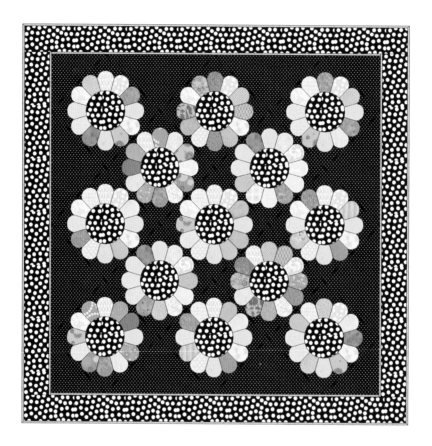

SUGGESTED LAYOUT

For my virtual quilt I have set thirteen Dresden Sunflower blocks on point with side and corner setting triangles. The side setting triangles are cut from two 15½" (39.4cm) squares of fabric cut on both diagonals to yield a total of eight. The corner triangles are cut from two 8⅛" (20.6cm) squares cut once on the diagonal to yield a total of four. I've added a ¼" (6mm) finished flange in bright yellow (see page 29), a 3¼" (8.3cm) finished border in black polka dot and a final binding in the same bright yellow. The quilt finishes at a fraction under 50" x 50" (127 x 127cm).

For one block you will need

Finished block size: 10" (25.4cm) square

- Twelve different orange and golden yellow scraps for the 'blades' of the Dresden plate, approximately 3" x 6" (7.6 x 15.2cm) each
- One 6" (15.2cm) square large-scale black-and-white polka dot print for the centre
- One 10½" (26.7cm) square very small-scale black-and-white polka dot print for the black background
- Twelve 3" (7.6cm) squares and one 6" (15.2cm) square of lightweight fusible interfacing

Assembling the block

1. From the various orange and yellow scraps cut a total of twelve shapes using Dresden Sunflowers template A (see page 233).

2. Place one fabric blade on top of one small interfacing square, right side of fabric next to the glue side (the rough or shiny side), and pin in place.

3. Using the edge of the fabric as a guide sew around the curve top only using a ¼" (6mm) seam allowance and a slightly shorter than normal stitch length. Trim the edge of the interfacing level with the curved edge.

4. Turn the interfacing to the back of the blade, so that the wrong sides of the fabric and interfacing are touching; this will turn the curved raw edge under. Use a point turner or chopstick to smooth the curve. Finger press (do not use an iron). Repeat for the remaining eleven blades.

5. Sew three of the blades together. Make four units like this and then sew the units into pairs. Finally sew the pairs together. Press the seams one way.

6. Fold the background square into quarters and finger press it lightly. Use the creases to help you position the ring of blades in the centre. Pin then appliqué in place, either by hand or machine.

7. Prepare the centre circle by cutting one circle from the large-scale black-and-white polka dot fabric using Dresden Sunflowers template B (see page 233) and the large square of interfacing. Place the fabric against the glue side of the interfacing and pin. Sew around the

fabric shape using a ¼" (6mm) seam allowance, then trim the excess interfacing from the edge. Snip the back of the interfacing, then turn to the right side (see page 24). Use a point turner or chopstick to smooth out the curved edge. Finger press, then pin in place in the centre of your block.

8. Appliqué the circle in place by hand or machine.

DRUNKARD'S PATH

Curved piecing attracts attention, admiration and fear in equal measure. Don't be put off by sewing curves – a little care and a few pins are all that is required to produce beautiful results! Make a monochromatic colour scheme so much more interesting by substituting various shades of grey for some of the black, and pale lilacs, golds and mint greens for the usual white.

For one block you will need

Finished block size:

12" (30.5cm) square

- Sixteen different scraps of assorted light cream/gold/white/ lilac and mint solids
- Eight different grey solids
- Black solid

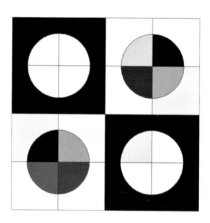

Assembling the block

1. From the assorted light solids, cut a total of eight quarter circles and eight backgrounds using Drunkard's Path templates A and B (see page 233).

2. From the various grey solids, cut a total of eight quarter circles and from the black solid cut a total of eight backgrounds, again using templates A and B.

3. Fold the quarter circles lightly in half, straight edges together, and finger press a crease in the edge. Do the same with the background pieces. These creases will help you to match the shapes accurately.

4. Match the creases up and pin the shapes right sides together. Match the ends and pin, then pin in between. Sew the seam with a ¼" (6mm) seam allowance.

5. Press the seams towards the darker fabric to complete the first Drunkard's Path unit.

6. Make a total of sixteen units, then sew them together in rows.

7. Sew the rows together to complete the block.

If curved piecing really doesn't appeal, you could follow my directions for fusible interfacing appliqué (page 24) and appliqué the quarter circles to 3½" (8.9cm) squares of background fabric instead.

SUGGESTED LAYOUT

For my virtual quilt I set sixteen blocks together to create a checkerboard with its own readymade 'border'. I added a 1" (2.5cm) finished border in black and bound the quilt with pale mint solid. The quilt finishes at 50" x 50" (127 x 127cm).

47

SPLIT STAR

I love to split blocks into half light and half dark if I possibly can and then, just like a Log Cabin block, I can start playing with the arrangement to create all kinds of secondary designs. A classic Variable Star gets divided across the diagonal and a great new block is created! I have used a collection of indigo blues and tans here, but any light/dark combo is sure to look wonderful.

For one block you will need

Finished block size: 9" (22.9cm) square

- One indigo print: cut one 3½" (8.9cm) square, two 4¼" (8.9cm) squares and two 3⅞"(9.8cm) squares
- One tan print: cut one 3½" (8.9cm) square, two 4¼" (8.9cm) squares and two 3⅞" (9.8cm) squares

Assembling the block

1. Pair up one tan and one indigo 4¼" (8.9cm) square right sides together and mark both diagonals, creating four marked triangles. Sew a ¼" (6mm) seam on the right-hand side of each of the marked triangles, as shown. Cut apart on the drawn lines. Make one more, creating a total of eight units. Sew pairs together to make the four quarter square triangle (QST) units as shown. See also page 19.
2. Pair one tan and one indigo 3⅞" (9.8cm) square right sides together and mark one diagonal. Sew a ¼" (6mm) seam allowance on either side of this marked line and then cut apart on the marked line to create two half square triangle (HST) units. Make one more. One of the HST units is spare.
3. Arrange the 3½" (8.9cm) squares, HST units and QST units to make the block, as shown.
4. Sew the units into rows and the rows together to finish the block.

Look at Log Cabin quilts to inspire you to try different settings for these blocks. Variations known as Streak o' Lightning, Straight Furrows and Sunshine and Shadows are all popular variations and would work with these blocks.

SUGGESTED LAYOUT

My virtual quilt contains sixteen Split Star blocks arranged in a 4 x 4 setting known as Barn Raising, but you could arrange them in a number of different configurations. I have added a 1" (2.5cm) finished border in tan, a 3" (7.6cm) finished border in indigo and a final 1" (2.5cm) finished tan border. The quilt finishes at 46" x 46" (116.8 x 116.8cm).

48 LOG CABIN WITH APPLIQUÉ

A Log Cabin quilt has been on my bucket list for years... it's one of the quintessential quilts that every quilter needs to make! I dug into my stash and found the richest, darkest and most luscious prints and batiks that I could find (there were many, but that's good – remember, more is more!). I teamed this deep palette with tans, creams and ivory tone on tones to create a quilt with high contrast. This created the perfect background for some invisible machine appliqué in the centre. Leave this off if you like; it's still a beautiful quilt – but if you've ever fancied a go at appliqué, here's your chance!

SUGGESTED LAYOUT

For my quilt I made a total of sixteen Log Cabin blocks and sewed them together in a 4 x 4 arrangement. I added a 1" (2.5cm) finished border and a final 6" (15.2cm) finished piano-key border made up of 1½" x 6½" (3.8 x 16.5cm) strips of dark/medium prints. The corner blocks on this final border are cut from the same black print used in the Log Cabin blocks and finish at 6" (15.2cm) square. The finished quilt is 78" x 78" (198 x 198cm).

For one block you will need

Finished block size:
16" (40.7cm) square

- One 2½" (6.4cm) square of black print for the block centre
- Fourteen strips of assorted dark scraps, each 1½" (3.8cm) wide and 2½"–15½" (6.4–39.4cm) long
- Fourteen strips of assorted cream/tans scraps, each 1½" (3.8cm) wide and 3½"–16½" (8.9–42cm) long

Spray starch your fabrics before you start cutting to make them a little firmer and easier to handle. This works really well to prevent distortion of your carefully pieced blocks!

LOG CABIN

48

Assembling the block

1. Starting with the centre 2½" (6.4cm) square, sew a 1½" x 2½" (3.8 x 6.4cm) dark print strip to the top and press the seam out towards the strip just added.
2. Add a 3½" (8.9cm) strip of dark print to the right-hand edge.
3. Add a 3½" (8.9cm) strip of cream/tan to the bottom and then a 4½" (11.4cm) strip of cream/tan to the left-hand edge.
4. Repeat these rounds following the same sequence of colours. The strips in round two are 4½" (11.4cm), 5½" (14cm), 5½" (14cm), 6½" (16.5cm).
5. The strips in round three are 6½" (16.5cm), 7½" (19cm), 7½" (19cm) and 8½" (21.6cm). Continue in this fashion adding rounds up to round seven, which should finish with a 16½" (42cm) strip of cream/tan.

APPLIQUÉ (optional)

Once the quilt top is completed, add the appliqué. You can use your favourite method of appliqué. I used the starch and press method detailed on page 24. Prepare the following for appliqué, using the templates on page 234: twenty-eight small leaves, four large leaves and four reverse large leaves, four large blossoms, four large blossom middles and four large blossom centres, five large circles, five medium circles and nine small circles. Also prepare approximately 65" (165cm) of ⅜" (10mm) wide bias stems. Appliqué the shapes in the following order: large leaves, reverse large leaves, stems, large, medium and small circles, large blossoms, blossom middles and centres, small circles, small leaves. Refer to the photograph on page 125.

BLOSSOM TRAIL

String-pieced segments of this quilt block make it the perfect option if you have lots of thin scraps that won't do for anything else. Sewing scraps together to create 'new' fabric expands the options and allows larger blocks to be created with the most meagre of scraps.

SUGGESTED LAYOUT

For my virtual quilt I have sewn together eighteen pink and twelve grey blocks and put them together in six rows of five. The quilt has a final binding in pink and finishes at 80" x 96" (203.2 x 243.8cm).

For one block you will need

Finished block size:

16" (40.7cm) square

- Assorted scraps of various pink prints at least ¾" x 12" (19mm x 30.5cm)
- Two 1" x 12" (2.5 x 30.5cm) scraps of medium grey
- One 9½" (24.1cm) square pink print, cut once on the diagonal to yield two triangles

Assembling the block

1. Start by sewing the various pink strips together to create a string-pieced panel that is at least 12" x 24"/30.5 x 61cm (see page 18).
2. Download and print (see page 224 for link) or photocopy one copy of Blossom Trail foundation A (see page 234) and use the strip-pieced unit to cover patch number one. Continue to piece the block using the paper foundation method (see page 21) then trim to 16½" x 16½" (42 x 42cm). Leave the paper intact until all the blocks have been sewn together.

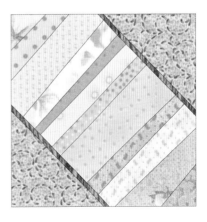

50 STICKS AND STONES

Simple to piece but packing a massive punch thanks to the combination of purple and lime green, my Sticks and Stones quilt consists of two easy blocks that will put a huge dent in your stash of 2½" (6.4cm) strips. I've gone for a two-colour quilt but a combination of medium/darks teamed with lights would make for a stunning quilt, too.

For one Sticks block you will need
Finished block size: 10" (25.4cm) square
- Five 2½" x 10½" (6.4 x 26.7cm) strips, three lime green and two purple

Assembling the Sticks block
1. Sew the strips together, alternating the colours. Press the seams towards the purple fabrics.

For one Stones block you will need
Finished block size: 10" (25.4cm) square
- Thirteen purple scraps, each 2½" (6.4cm) square
- Twelve lime green scraps, each 2½" (6.4cm) square

Assembling the Stones block
1. Lay the squares out in a 5 x 5 arrangement, alternating the colours.
2. Sew the rows together, pressing the seams towards the purple fabrics.
3. Sew the rows together and press the seams open.

SUGGESTED LAYOUT

For my virtual quilt I have teamed seventeen Stones blocks with thirty-two Sticks blocks to create a 70" x 70" (177.8 x 177.8cm) quilt.

Try substituting the purple scraps for an assortment of 1930s reproduction prints and omit the Sticks blocks, substituting a solid light blue. Add appliqué flowers in the alternate blocks for a beautiful and very different variation.

51 COURTHOUSE STEPS

Some quilt blocks are so timeless that they have an enduring appeal to quilters both modern and traditional. Courthouse Steps fits that bill for me, as at home in a log cabin in the prairies as it would be in a New York loft. My version uses warm and rich country-style fabrics, but solids in shades of teal, lime and grey would look amazing, too.

For one block you will need

Finished block size:
11" (28cm) square

- Four 1½" (3.8cm) squares in assorted dark prints
- Twenty-one 1½" (3.8cm) squares in assorted light prints
- Sixteen assorted dark strips, 1½" (3.8cm) wide in the following lengths: four 3½" (8.9cm), four 5½" (14cm), four 7½" (19cm), four 9½" (24.1cm)

Assembling the block

1. Sew the four dark print 1½" (3.8cm) squares together with five of the light 1½" (3.8cm) squares to make the block centre, as shown.
2. Sew a 3½" (8.9cm) dark strip to opposite sides of the centre and press seams towards the strips.
3. Sew a 1½" (3.8cm) light square to each end of the remaining two 3½" (8.9cm) dark strips and press the seams towards the dark strips. Sew these strips to the remaining opposite sides of the block centre.
4. Continue to add rounds to the centre until all four rounds have been completed.

Don't be afraid to join two or more smaller scraps of the same fabric together in order to achieve some of the longer lengths of strip needed for this quilt.

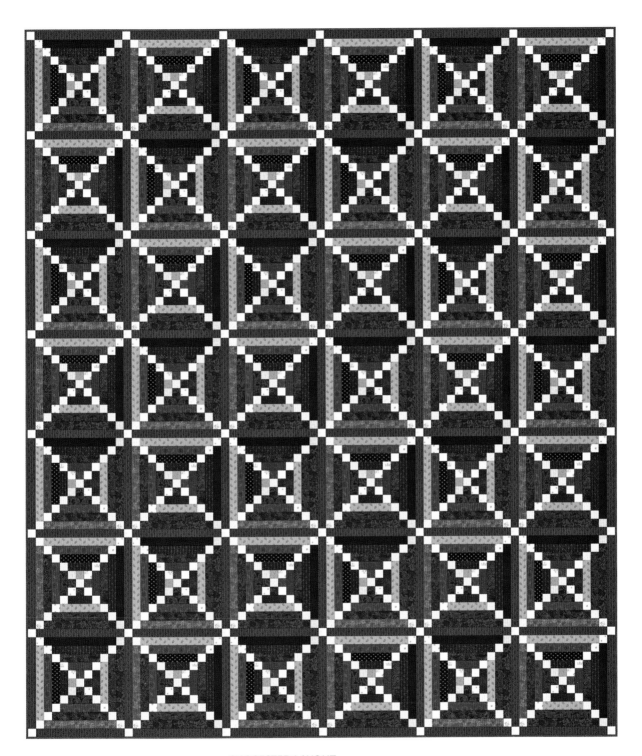

SUGGESTED LAYOUT

For my virtual quilt I have set forty-two blocks in seven rows of six with 1" (2.5cm) wide finished sashing strips in a dark print and 1" (2.5cm) finished cornerstones in a variety of light prints. The quilt finishes at 73" x 85" (185.4 x 216cm) – a great size for a single bed.

LINKED

A combination of simple squares and Drunkard's Path units creates a striking modern block that looks much harder than it actually is! Isn't that the best? A background of grey prints helps to make the lime greens pop without being overly harsh.

For one block you will need
Finished block size:
10" (25.4cm) square
- Nine scraps of assorted grey prints cut into 2½" (6.4cm) squares
- Four scraps of assorted grey prints cut using background template A
- Eight scraps of assorted grey prints cut using quarter circle template B
- Four scraps of assorted green prints cut into 2½" (6.4cm) squares
- Eight scraps of assorted green prints cut using background template A
- Four scraps of assorted green prints cut using quarter circle template B
See page 235 for templates

Assembling the block
1.   Make eight Drunkard's Path units using grey quarter circles and green backgrounds.
2.   Make four Drunkard's Path units using grey backgrounds and green quarter circles.
3.   Arrange the Drunkard's Path units and the squares into five rows of five, using the diagram above as a guide.
4.   Sew the units into five rows, then join the rows.

I like to use a small wooden roller to 'press' my seams when doing curved piecing.

SUGGESTED LAYOUT

For my virtual quilt I set sixteen Linked blocks together in four rows of four giving me a finished quilt of 40" x 40" (101.6 x 101.6cm) – this would make a terrific wall quilt.

STAINED GLASS WINDOW

The humble half square triangle is the foot soldier of the quilting world. Unsung and overlooked, it is remarkably versatile and in this quilt, it gets to be the hero!

For one block you will need

Finished block size: 6" (15.2cm) square

- Sixteen assorted light scraps cut into 1⅞" (4.8cm) squares
- Sixteen dark grey 1⅞" (4.8cm) squares
- Eight dark grey 1½" (3.8cm) squares

Assembling the block

1. Pair up one light scrap and one dark grey 1⅞" (4.8cm) square, right sides together and mark the diagonal on the back of the light square. Sew ¼" (6mm) either side of this line, then cut apart to create two half square triangle (HST) units. Make a total of thirty-two HST units (see page 19).
2. Arrange the HST units and the eight dark grey 1½" (3.8cm) squares to form the block, using the diagram as a guide. Sew the units into rows.
3. Sew the rows together.

I like to use heat-resistant batting (wadding) in my table runners so that hot dishes will not damage the table underneath. Heat resistant batting can shift when quilting, so I use a basting spray (505 spray is ideal) to hold the layers together before I quilt.

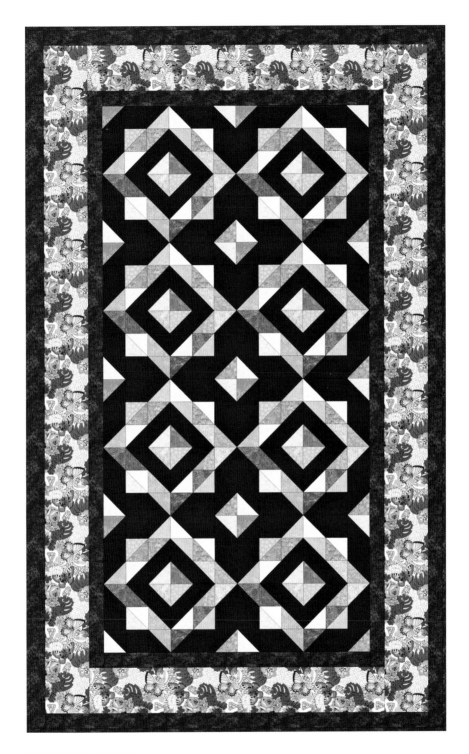

SUGGESTED LAYOUT

For my virtual quilt I have set eight blocks in two rows of four to create a table runner. I've added a 1" (2.5cm) finished border in dark grey, a 3" (7.6cm) finished border in lilac and a final 1" (2.5cm) finished border in dark grey to frame the piece. The table runner finishes at 22" x 34" (55.8 x 86.3cm).

54 HONEY BEE

This is my version of the classic Honey Bee block. I've altered the appliqués slightly to create a more interesting secondary pattern where the blocks meet. Use your favourite method to appliqué by hand or machine.

For one block you will need

Finished block size: 13" (33cm) square

- Five 3½" (8.9cm) squares of assorted red and pink prints
- Four 3½" (8.9cm) squares of solid red
- Four 2½" x 9½" (6.4 x 24.1cm) rectangles of solid pink
- Four 2½" (6.4cm) squares of solid pink
- Twelve scraps of assorted red and pink prints cut using template A honey bee (see page 235)

Assembling the block

1. Sew the five print and four red solid 3½" (8.9cm) squares together in three rows of three to make the centre nine patch.

2. Sew a 2½" x 9½" (6.4 x 24.1cm) pink solid rectangle to one side of the nine patch, then press the seams towards the rectangle. Add another rectangle to the opposite side of the nine patch.

3. Sew a 2½" (6.4cm) pink solid square to each end of the remaining two 2½" x 9½" (6.4 x 24.1cm) rectangles.

4. Sew the units made in step 3 to the two remaining sides of the nine patch. Press the seams towards the outer rectangles.

5. Prepare the appliqué shapes for fused or turned edge appliqué using your preferred method (see pages 24–26). Appliqué three shapes to each corner of the block, butting the shapes together at the inner corner and ensuring that there is a ¼" (6mm) left at the outer seam allowances.

Use a variety of cheerful 1930s reproduction prints and white solids in place of my reds and pinks for a very pretty version. If you're making this quilt for a bed, I recommend using a turned-edge appliqué method for durability.

SUGGESTED LAYOUT

For my virtual quilt I have set sixteen Honey Bee blocks together in four rows of four separated by 1" (2.5cm) finished sashing in solid red and 1" (2.5cm) finished cornerstones in a pale aqua solid. I have varied the value of the background solids in the blocks – some are light pink and some medium pink. There is a ¼" (6mm) flange border in pale aqua (see page 29) and a final 1" (2.5cm) finished border, bringing the quilt to a finished size of 59" x 59" (150 x 150cm).

MAGIC BEANSTALK

I love to appliqué and it's a fabulous and often overlooked way to use scraps! Joining your scraps together by machine before you cut the appliqués reduces construction time and makes the whole job easier. The centre stalk is pieced, making the blocks easy to handle and very portable... a great project to have in your bag for when you have five spare minutes. You'll be amazed how fast this beanstalk grows!

For one block you will need

Finished block size: 13" (33cm) square

- Twelve assorted scraps for the leaf appliqués, approximately 5" x 2" (12 x 5cm) in various shades of green, purple, orange and pink
- One strip of vibrant green print 1½" x 13½" (3.8 x 34.3cm)
- Two rectangles of tan solid for the appliqué background, each 4½" x 13½" (11.4 x 34.3cm)
- Two rectangles of purple print for the block edges, each 2½" x 13½" (6.4 x 34.3cm)

Assembling the block

1. Take two contrasting 5" x 2" (12 x 3cm) scraps and sew them together along one long edge to make a rectangle measuring 5" x 4" (12 x 10cm). Press the seam open. From this joined scrap and centring the seam on the centre of the template, cut out one leaf shape using Magic Beanstalk appliqué template (page 235). Use your favourite method of appliqué (see pages 24–26) but remember if you are doing turned-edge appliqué you will need to add your own turn under allowance. For fused appliqué, apply fusible web to the back of the joined rectangle first, then cut out the appliqué shape.
2. Join the two tan background rectangles to each side of the vibrant green 'stem' and press the seams towards the stem. Join the purple block edgings to each side of the background unit and press the seams towards the purple edge.
3. Appliqué three leaves to either side of the 'stem' using your preferred method. Make sure that the leaves touch the stem and the edge but do not overlap.

Include some single-colour leaves for variety and if you like you could add some appliqué ladybugs and butterflies. As a variation, why not make one vertical row of blocks and add a fabric tape measure to the side. Attached to the wall, it would make a fantastic growth chart for your own little giants!

SUGGESTED LAYOUT

For my virtual quilt I have joined twenty Magic Beanstalk blocks together with vertical bright green sashing. I have added two borders – the first a 1" (2.5cm) finished border in the same bright green as the sashing, and the second a 3" (7.6cm) finished border in the same purple that I used in the blocks. The finished quilt is 63" x 73" (160 x 185.4cm).

56 REFLECTED

Clean lines and vibrant colours meet in a striking quilt made of one simple block, with half blocks to stagger the rows. A design wall is useful for arranging the various blocks until the perfect setting is found. Take photographs as you arrange the blocks, as it's often easier to see when something is 'right' or 'wrong' in a photograph.

SUGGESTED LAYOUT

For my virtual quilt I have set thirty-three full blocks and six half blocks together in rows, the half blocks appearing at the top and bottom of the second, fourth and sixth rows to offset the blocks. I have added a 1" (2.5cm) finished border in very dark grey and a grey binding. The finished quilt is 56" x 74" (142.2 x 190.5cm).

If you need to supplement your scraps, consider a 'fabric exchange' with a friend. Swap similar sized pieces – e.g. 10" (25.4cm) squares or 2½" (6.4cm) strips – to expand your stash without spending a penny!

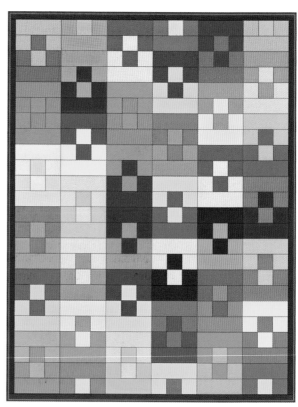

For one block you will need

Finished block size: 9" x 12" (22.9 x 30.5cm)

- Two contrasting solid scraps. From each solid cut the following pieces: three 3½" (8.9cm) squares and one 3½" x 9½" (8.9 x 23.5cm) rectangle

Assembling the block

1. Sew three 3½" (8.9cm) squares together, alternating the colours. Repeat with the remaining three 3½" (8.9cm) squares.
2. Sew the two rows of joined squares together to make a checkerboard unit.
3. Sew the remaining rectangles to the top and bottom of the unit, paying close attention to the colour placement.

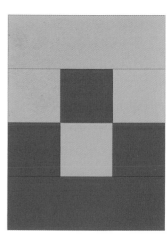

HIGH SPEED TWO

Half square triangles, often referred to as HSTs, are such a speedy block to make, especially when you follow my method on page 19. This quilt will whip up in no time!

SUGGESTED LAYOUT

For my virtual quilt I made a total of thirty-six units. I added a 1" (2.5cm) finished frame of dark red, then bound the quilt in the same colour to make a quilt that finishes at 56" x 56" (142.2 x 142.2cm).

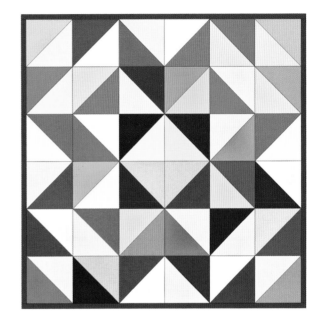

You will need

Finished block size: 9" (22.9cm) square
- Eighteen 10" (25.4cm) squares of bright/dark solids
- Eighteen 10" (25.4cm) squares of light/pastel solids

Assembling the block

1. Pair one bright/dark solid 10" (25.4cm) square with one light/pastel 10" square, right sides together, and draw the diagonal lightly with pencil.
2. Sew ¼" (6mm) either side of the pencil line.
3. Cut apart on the drawn line to create two half square triangle (HST) units. Press the seams towards the dark side.
4. Trim the unit to 9½" (24.1cm) square, making sure that the diagonal runs through the middle.

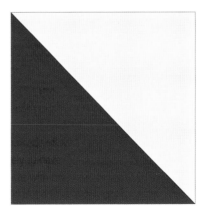

I like to make my HST units slightly larger than I need them and trim them to size. A large square ruler is brilliant for squaring up.

58 CROSSED BRANCHES

I love the combination of pumpkin orange and federal blue – and when you mix those ingredients with a bounty of tan and cream prints, a bunch of appliqués and Flying Geese sashing, you have a winner!

For one block you will need

Finished block size:
18" (45.7cm) square

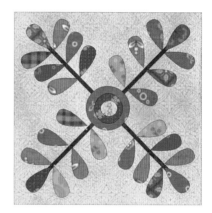

- Twenty-eight small scraps for the leaf appliqués in shades of deep rust, pumpkin, red and federal blue
- Three scraps for the centre circles
- 40" (101.6cm) of ⅜" (10mm) bias stem made in dark brown print (made from one ¾"/19mm strip of fabric)
- One 20" (50.8cm) square of cream/tan print for the block background

Assembling the block

1. Prepare the appliqués using your chosen method. The templates are on page 235. Follow the general instructions for fused, interfaced or starch and press appliqué (see pages 24–26).
2. Lightly fold the background square on both diagonals and gently crease with your fingers.
3. Use the creases to position and appliqué the stems in place then appliqué the leaves and finally the centre circles.
4. Trim the block to 18½" x 18½" (47 x 47cm), centring the design.

Pre-starch and iron dry your 'stem' fabric before you cut it into ¾" (19mm) strips. The extra firmness will make it go through your bias tape maker much more easily and the stem will retain its folded edges while you sew.

SUGGESTED LAYOUT

For my virtual quilt I have set nine blocks in three rows of three, separated by Flying Geese sashing. The sashing segments are each 6" x 18" (15.2 x 45.7cm) finished and consist of six Flying Geese units made with the 'no-waste' method (see page 20). The 'goose' fabric is cut at 7¼" x 7¼" (18.4 x 18.4cm) and the four squares of 'sky' at 3⅞" (9.8cm), giving a total of four geese units. The cornerstones are made from 6½" (16.5cm) squares of various tan prints. Border 1 in federal blue finishes at 1" (2.5cm), border 2 at 4" (10.2cm) and border 3 at 1" (2.5cm). The finished quilt measures 90" (228.6cm) square, perfect for a queen or double bed.

NEW YORK IN THE SPRING

New York Beauty blocks have always held a fascination for me... I just love the spiky points and the gorgeous curves. The combination of fresh spring green and turquoise reminded me of Central Park in the sunshine. Two different variations offer even more scrappy possibilities!

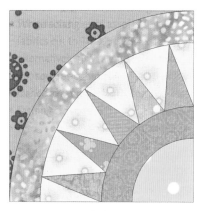

Block A

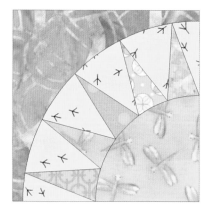

Block B

To make one block you will need

Finished block size: 10" (25.4cm) square
- Five different bright greens for the 'rays'
- Assorted light green scraps for the quarter circle and arcs

Assembling the blocks

1. Download and print (see page 224 for link) or photocopy the templates for either block A or block B. You will need one copy of New York in the Spring foundation A and one copy of the remaining templates (see page 236).
2. Following the general instructions for paper foundation piecing (page 21), piece the rays (see page 21). Trim to within the ¼" (6mm) seam line.
3. Use the remaining paper pieces as templates to cut the arcs and quarter circle.
4. Sew the arcs and quarter-circle to the foundation-pieced rays section as shown. Remove the papers.

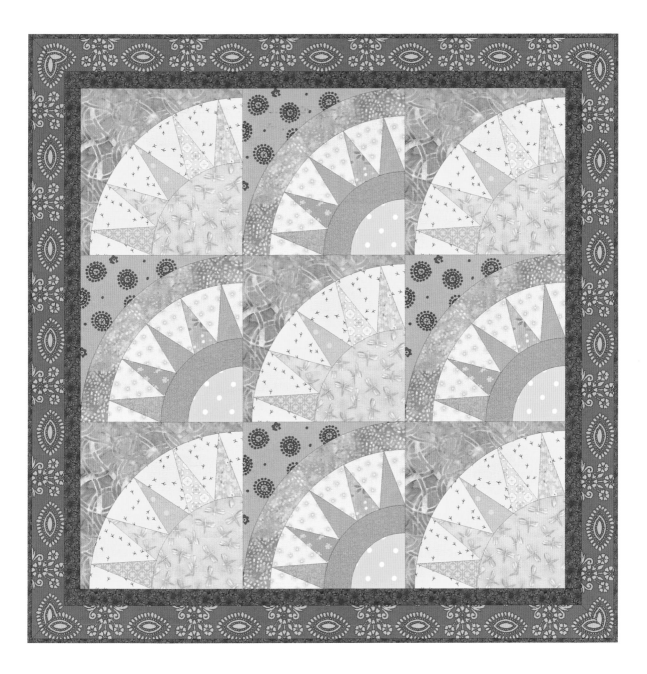

If you don't like to remove paper when you foundation piece, you could trace the foundation patterns onto lightweight sew-in interfacing. The interfacing remains in the block and does not need to be removed.

SUGGESTED LAYOUT

For my virtual quilt I made four block As and five block Bs and pieced them together in three rows of three. Border 1 finishes at 1" (2.5cm) and border 2 finishes at 2" (5.1cm). The quilt is 36" x 36" (91.4 x 91.4cm).

60 CRAZY FOR QUILTING

Crazy patchwork blocks are the obvious choice for a collection of odd-sized and -shaped scraps. I've chosen to work in one colour, but you could just throw everything you've got at this one. Traditionally the seam lines would be decorated with hand or machine embroidery. Perhaps this is the opportunity to try out some of those decorative stitches your fancy machine can do? To keep the block stable and in shape, I recommend using the 'stitch and flip' method onto a calico backing.

For one block you will need
Finished block size: 9" (22.9cm) square
- One 10" (25.4cm) square of calico
- Seven–twelve assorted scraps

Assembling the block
1. Start with a four-, five- or six-sided shape, cut roughly with scissors or a rotary cutter and placed somewhere near the middle of the calico square, right side up.
2. Place your second scrap right side down on the first shape and sew down one edge with a ¼" (6mm) seam allowance.
3. Flip the second patch back to the right side and press.
4. Continue to add patches to the centre shape, working in a clockwise direction until the whole piece of calico is covered. You may have to trim the patches to shape as you go.
5. Trim the block to 9½" x 9½" (24.1 x 24.1cm).

For variety, you could sew two or three fabrics together and treat them as one patch. This helps to prevent every block looking the same.

SUGGESTED LAYOUT

My virtual quilt is made up of thirty blocks set in a five rows of six arrangement. This makes a quilt top that finishes at 45" x 54" (114.3 x 137.2cm) – a great size for a sofa throw. The calico makes the top thicker, so I would highly recommend a thin quilt batting (wadding) and machine quilting. Hand quilting might be just a bit too challenging through all those layers!

CASTELLATED

Inspired by the castellated tops of medieval castles and Victorian follies, this is an easy quilt to piece and a huge amount of fun. Play with the placement of lights and darks; they do not always appear in the same part of the block and the arrangement will be so much more fun if you mirror this in your placement. This is a great quilt for using up those fat quarters you just couldn't resist!

For one block you will need
Finished block size:
18" (45.7cm) square
- Four different scraps. From each scrap cut four 3½" (8.9cm) squares and one 3½" x 18½" (8.9 x 47cm) rectangle

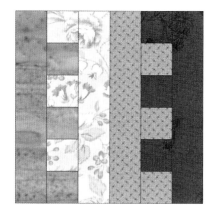

Assembling the block

1. Pair up your chosen scraps. Sew the squares together in a row, alternating the colours. Sew a corresponding rectangle to each long edge.
2. Make another unit as in step 1 using the other two scraps.
3. Sew the two pieced units together, using the diagram above as a guide to placement.

I love using striped fabrics for sashings and bindings – they are worth so much more than the sum of their parts and add a dynamic finish to even the simplest of quilts.

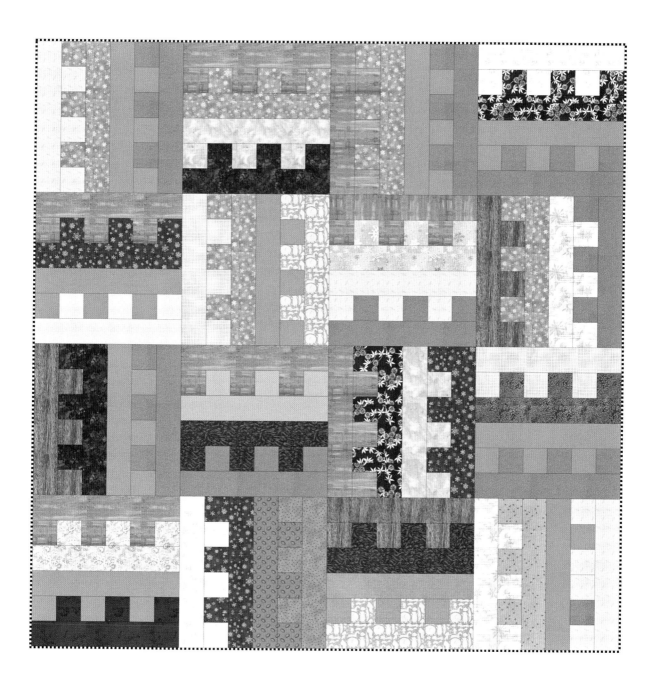

SUGGESTED LAYOUT

My virtual quilt uses sixteen blocks set in four rows of four. Each alternate block is twisted 90 degrees to create a quilt with lots of movement. The quilt finishes at 72" x 72" (182.8 x 182.8cm) and I've used a black-and-white stripe binding to echo the piecing.

ROUNDABOUT

Who doesn't love a strip roll? Since Moda introduced the first 'jelly rolls' those 2½" (6.4cm) strip bundles have been driving quilters crazy with desire. There are often a few strips left over and to these I add my leftovers from binding quilts (rather conveniently 2½"/6.4cm strips!) and anything else I have laying around. This quilt is so fast to make it feels like cheating. It's not – it's great! Particularly when you have to make a quilt in a hurry!

SUGGESTED LAYOUT

For my finished 60" (152.4cm) square quilt, all that was left to do was to layer and quilt. How fast would it be to make a king-sized quilt using four Roundabout blocks stitched in two rows of two?

You will need

Finished block/quilt size: 60" (152.4cm) square

- Forty 2½" x 42" (6.4 x 106.7cm) strips of assorted prints and solids (I used half and half)
- One 20½" (52cm) square of a multi-coloured print that pulls all your strip colours together

Assembling the block

1. Choose ten of your strips. I laid all my chosen colours out first and grouped them into ten sets of four. Each set of four had similar colourings.
2. Sew the ten strips together to make a panel 20½" x 42" (52 x 106.7cm), then press the seams one way.
3. Trim the panel to 40½" (102.9cm) long (20½"/52cm wide).
4. Make a total of four strip-pieced panels.
5. Sew the first strip-pieced panel to one side of the centre 20½" (52cm) square, but only sew the first 10" (25.4cm) as shown (seam 1).
6. Sew the next strip-pieced panel to the next adjacent side of the centre square (seam 2).
7. Continue to add the strip-pieced panels (seam 3 and 4). When you have added the final panel you will be able to complete the very first, partial seam (seam 5).
8. Press the seams outwards as you go.

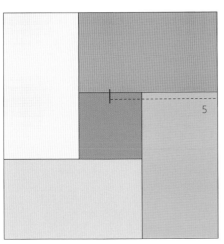

If you don't have a 20½" (52cm) square for the centre of the quilt, why not piece a centre? One hundred 2½" (6.4cm) squares stitched in a 10 x 10 arrangement would be spectacular, or you could sew sixteen 5" (12.7cm) finished half square triangle units or quarter square triangle units (see page 19) together.

CROSSED CANOES

If you've never tried paper foundation piecing, before I would really encourage you to give it a go! Follow the general instructions on page 21 and make this classic block. I wouldn't attempt it any other way!

SUGGESTED LAYOUT

My virtual quilt is 58" x 58" (147.3 x 147.3cm) and is composed of twenty blocks. Sixteen of them make the quilt centre, arranged in four rows of four. I've then added a 1" (2.5cm) finished border in bright orange, a 9" (22.9cm) finished border in teal, and a further four Crossed Canoes blocks at the corners and a final 1" (2.5cm) finished orange border to frame and finish the quilt.

When foundation paper piecing, keep a roll of clear tape handy in case you need to repair the foundation.

For one block you will need

Finished block size: 9" (22.9cm) square

- Three different orange prints
- Three different teal prints
- Four different ivory prints

Assembling the block

1. Download and print (see page 224 for link) or photocopy four copies of the Crossed Canoe foundation (see page 237).
2. Following the general instructions, page 21, piece the four units, trimming the seam allowances as you go.
3. Sew the units together. Leave the paper intact until all the blocks have been sewn together.

MEXICAN FIESTA

Bring the warmth, vibrancy and colour of a Mexican fiesta to your sewing room with this foundation-pieced beauty. Let all your most colourful scraps play together with just a touch of purple to contrast and contain the fiesta!

SUGGESTED LAYOUT

For my virtual quilt I have set sixty-three Mexican Fiesta blocks in seven rows of nine, separated with ½" (12mm) finished sashing in a rich, warm purple batik. I have included a sashed border, border 2 finishes at 2" (5.1cm) and the final purple border also finishes at ½" (12mm). The final binding is in an orange/red print batik. The quilt is 51" x 64" (129.5 x 162.6cm).

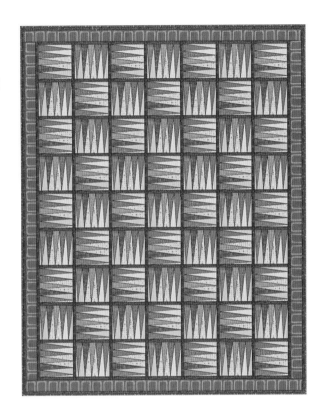

When adding borders or long pieces of sashing to a quilt, cut your fabric on the lengthwise grain if you possibly can. This is the most stable and least stretchy grain of the fabric and will help prevent your quilt edges from wobbling.

For one block you will need

Finished block size: 6" (15.2cm) square

- Five assorted scraps of vibrant orange and red prints/solids/batiks, at least 2" x 7" (5.1 x 17.8cm)
- Six assorted yellow scraps, at least 3" x 7" (7.6 x 17.8cm)

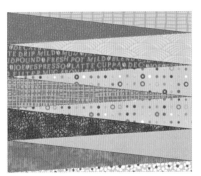

Assembling the block

1. Download and print (see page 224 for link) or photocopy one copy of Mexican Fiesta foundation A (see page 237).
2. Following the general instructions on paper foundation piecing (page 21), piece the block in numerical order, trimming the seam allowances as you go.
3. Press and trim to 6½" x 6½" (16.5 x 16.5cm). Leave the paper intact until all the blocks have been sewn together.

KNITTED SQUARES

I've been knitting since I was three years old and I am always looking to my other crafts for inspiration. This quilt came from a knitted swatch that I found and it really does prove what many quilters already know: 'red is a neutral!' Mix a variety of red solids in various values with assorted print scraps for a dazzling magic carpet of a quilt. The strips are narrow but the blocks are big, so the quilt is not as daunting as you might first think!

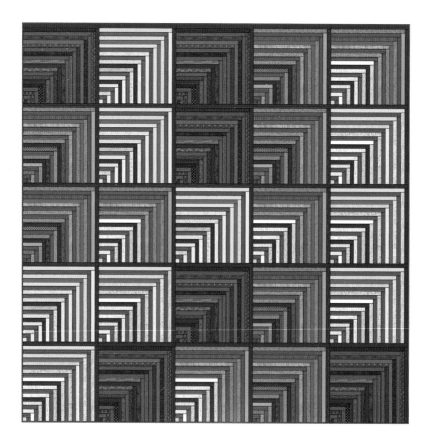

SUGGESTED LAYOUT

For my virtual quilt I have used a variety of browns, yellows, blues and rust print scraps mixed with various shades of red solids. I've arranged twenty-five blocks in five rows of five making a quilt that finishes at 100" x 100" (254 x 254cm). The final binding is in a dark red solid.

For one block you will need

Finished block size: 20" (50.8cm) square

- Various red solid strips, each cut 1½" (3.8cm) wide and varying in length from 1½" (3.8cm) up to 20½" (52cm)
- Various print fabric strips, each cut 1½" (3.8cm) wide and varying in length from 1½" (3.8cm) to 19½" (49.5cm)

Assembling the block

1. The block is essentially a partial Log Cabin and is made in much the same way. Start with a 1½" (3.8cm) square of print fabric and sew first a 1½" (3.8cm) square and then a 1½" x 2½" (3.8 x 6.4cm) strip of red solid to two adjacent sides.

2. From this point on you will only add subsequent strips to these same two sides, so the block builds from the corner outwards. Add strips of print fabric at 1½" x 2½" (3.8 x 6.4cm) first, then add 1½" x 3½" (3.8 x 8.9cm).

3. Continue adding strips in this way, alternating between print strips and solid red strips, until your final red solid strips are cut at 19½" (49.5cm) and 20½" (52cm).

4. Seams should be pressed outwards as you go.

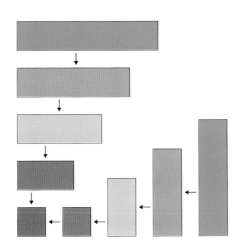

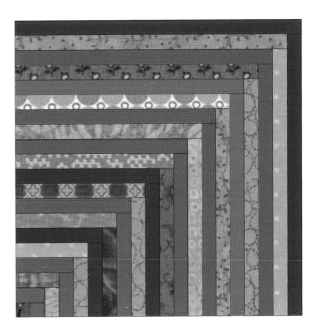

MACHINE-STITCHED CATHEDRAL WINDOW

Many quilters have tried cathedral window patchwork by hand, and I suspect most still have the project, unfinished, in a cupboard somewhere! My version is completely machine stitched: fast, fun and achievable! Traditionally this sort of quilt contained no batting (wadding), but I have included a very thin cotton batting for extra loft and warmth.

SUGGESTED LAYOUT

For my quilt I cut 144 pastel squares and laid them out in a 12 x 12 arrangement. I cut and folded 288 white 5" (12.7cm) squares and basted them on top of the pastel squares. I then joined the covered squares into 9" (22.9cm) blocks then joined the blocks together. I layered the quilt top with thin batting and backing fabric, cut 3" (7.6cm) bigger on all sides then pinned a further sixty-one pastel 5" (12.7cm) squares over the block intersections. Peel back the white edges of the folded squares and stitch in place – this catches the edges and quilts at the same time! Trim the batting and backing even with the quilt top then bind the edges of your quilt with a white solid.

For one block you will need

Finished block size: 9" (22.9cm) square

- Five squares of assorted pastel print fabrics cut to 5" (12.7cm)
- Eight squares of white solid fabric cut to 5" (12.7cm)

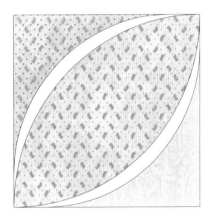

A lot of sewers don't like pinning or basting... they feel it slows them down. It actually ensures far greater accuracy and you are much less likely to have to unpick and re-stitch. Pinning and basting is a good thing! I baste with my machine stitch set at the maximum stitch length so it's easy to pull out if I need to. I baste about ⅛" (3mm) in from the raw edges so that, when I sew my seam 'for real', the basting will not be seen.

MACHINE-STITCHED CATHEDRAL WINDOW

Assembling the block

1. Start by pressing all of your white squares in half on the diagonal, wrong side to wrong side. Line up the edges of the fabric very accurately before you press!
2. Lay out four of your pastel print 5" (12.7cm) squares in two rows of two.
3. Lay the folded white squares on top of the pastel squares as shown. Pin, then machine baste the white squares on top of the pastel squares.
4. Sew the 'four patch' together.
5. If you peel back the edges of the white squares, the pastel underneath will be visible.
6. Pin the fifth pastel square, on point, on the centre of the block.
7. Pin the outer folded edges of the white squares. Fold the inner edges over the raw edges of the central square, and pin in place.
8. Start in the top left corner and sew down the four outer curved edges, then continue around the four inner curved edges, covering the raw edges of the centre pastel square as you stitch. Make sure you are sewing very close to the edge of the white fabric.

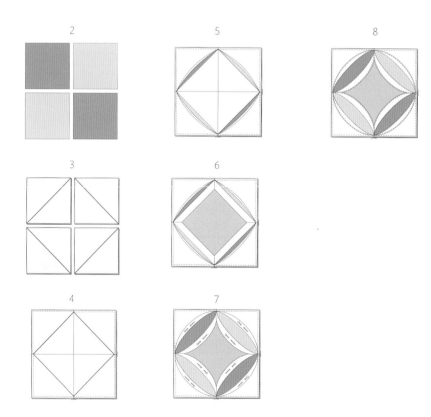

PLAID BARS

Most of us have fabrics that we can't or won't cut into, either for aesthetic or sentimental reasons. This quilt is a great way to use large pieces of fabric and protect the 'integrity' of each one. What a lovely project to use a loved one's collection of plaid shirts! You could even keep the button plackets intact on some of them.

You will need

Finished quilt size:
53½" x 54" (135.8 x 137.2cm)

- Forty rectangles of assorted plaid fabrics cut to 10" x 5" (25.4 x 12.7cm); alternatively use twenty layer cake 10" squares cut in half
- Dark brown print fabric for the sashing

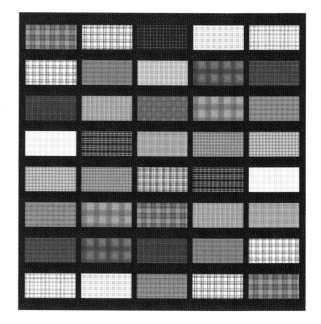

Assembling the quilt top

1. The vertical sashing is cut at 1½" (3.8cm) wide x 54" (137.2cm) long. You will need six pieces. The horizontal pieces are cut at 2½" (6.4cm) wide x 10" (25.4cm) long and you will need 45 pieces.
2. Arrange the plaid rectangles in eight rows of five with the 2½" x 10" (6.4 x 25.4cm) sashing pieces in between. Sew the rows.
3. Sew the 1½" x 53½" (3.8 x 135.9cm) sashing strips to either side of the vertical rows, then sew the rows together.

> If you are using old shirts to make this quilt, ensure that they are all of a similar weight and fibre content. You can make them all the same weight by fusing the lighter ones to fusible interfacing before you cut your rectangles.

68 SPOTS AND STRIPES

Sometimes you feel like doing some really precise and complex patchwork and sometimes the mood calls for something a little more liberated! Spots and stripes is a great example of 'liberated' piecing. Try it and you might just find yourself hooked!

SUGGESTED LAYOUT

For my virtual quilt I have set sixteen blocks together in four rows of four, twisting each alternate block a quarter turn. This adds movement and life to the quilt. I've added a 1" (2.5cm) finished border in solid black and a ¼" (6mm) flange in bright yellow (see page 27) before the black binding. The quilt finishes at 50" x 50" (127 x 127cm) and would make a very stimulating baby quilt.

For one block you will need

Finished block size: 12" (30.5cm) square

- Assorted small scraps in two different colour 'families', approximately six of each
- Black solid
- Large white dot on black fabric

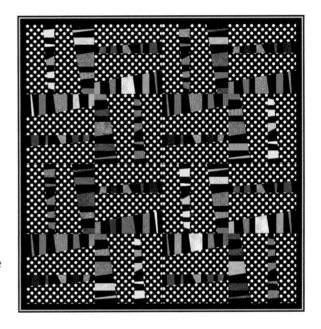

Assembling the block

1. Cut the assorted bright scraps into strips and wedges approximately 1–2" (2.5–5.1cm) wide and approximately 4" (10.2cm) long. Do the same with the black solid.
2. Sew the assorted bright scraps and black solid pieces together to create a panel approximately 4" x 13" (10.2 x 33cm), using one colour family at a time, as shown. Make another panel using a different colour family and more black solid.
3. Trim the panels into a 'wedge' shape approximately 4" (10.2cm) wide at one end and approximately 2½" (6.4cm) wide at the other.
4. Cut two pieces of black/white dot print into wedge shapes approximately 5½" (14cm) wide at one end, 3½" (8.9cm) wide at the other and 13" (33cm) long.
5. Sew the pieced and the plain wedges together. Square up your block to 12½" x 12½" (31.7 x 31.7cm).

CRAYON BOX STARS

For this block I've gone for a piecing challenge! Half square triangles in bright solids teamed with a variety of pale grey prints make a quilt that looks ultra modern but is very much a traditional style. That's the best of both worlds in my book!

For one block you will need

Finished block size:

15" (40.1cm) square

- Sixteen 2⅜" (6cm) squares in lightest grey print
- Four 2" (5.1cm) squares in lightest grey print
- One 4¼" (10.8cm) square in lightest grey print
- Two 3⅞" (9.8cm) squares in lightest grey print
- Four 2" x 9½" (5.1 x 24.1cm) rectangles in medium grey print
- Four 2" (5.1cm) squares in dark grey print
- Sixteen 2⅜" (6cm) squares in assorted bright solids
- Two 3⅞" (9.8cm) squares in assorted bright solids
- Three 4¼" (10.8cm) squares in assorted bright solids
- One 3½" (8.9cm) square in assorted bright solids

Assembling the block

1. Use the 2⅜" (6cm) light grey and assorted bright solid squares to make a total of 32 half square triangle (HST) units, using the method described on page 163.
2. Sew the HST units into four strips of eight HST units. Set aside.
3. Use the four 4¼" (10.8cm) squares to make a total of four quarter square triangle units (QST), following the general instructions on page 19. To achieve the correct colour combinations, pair your squares as shown, right.
4. Use the four 3⅞" (9.8cm) squares to make a total of four HST units, following the general instructions on page 19.
5. Assemble the block in rows, as shown, then sew the rows together.

Making half square triangles for this block needn't be a chore if you chain piece! Mark the diagonal lightly in pencil on the back of each light grey square. Stack your light grey and bright solid 2⅜" (6cm) squares next to your sewing machine. Sew the first pair ¼" (6mm) away from the marked diagonal, lift the presser foot of your machine, butt the next pair up to the first, lower the presser foot and continue sewing. Keep adding your squares in a 'chain'. When you get to the end, turn the whole strip of 'bunting' around and sew on the opposite side of your marked line. Set your seams, clip the squares apart and cut your squares apart on the drawn line. Press the seam allowances towards the bright solid. Half square triangles in record time!

SUGGESTED LAYOUT

My virtual quilt is 99" x 99" (251.4 x 251.4cm), a great size for a queen bed. The twenty-five blocks are set with 1½" (3.8cm) finished sashing and cornerstones. I've added five borders – each one finishes at 1½" (3.8cm) so cut the plain strips at 2" (5.1cm) and make a total of 236 HST units for border number four.

70 STARS AND CHAINS

Don't be alarmed by the odd-shaped star units. The stitch and flip method (see page 20) makes this block a breeze.

For one block you will need

Finished block size:

12" (30.5cm) square

- Four rectangles 2½" x 6½" (6.4cm x 16.5cm) in dark brown
- Eight 2½" (6.4cm) squares in pale grey
- Four rectangles 2½" x 4½" (6.4cm x 11.4cm) in coffee
- Four 4½" (11.4cm) squares in pale grey

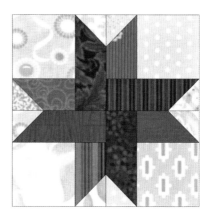

Assembling the Simple Star block

1. Take one 2½" x 6½" (6.4 x 16.5cm) dark brown rectangle. Take one 2½" (6.4cm) grey square and lightly mark the diagonal on the wrong side with a pencil. Place this small square, right sides together, on the top of the dark brown rectangle, with the diagonal line running from top left to bottom right. Pin, then stitch on the marked diagonal. Trim the corner away, flip the corner back and press. Make four identical units.

2. Take one 2½" x 4½" (6.4 x 11.4cm) coffee rectangle and one 2½" (6.4cm) grey square (again with the diagonal marked in pencil). Place the small square at the top of the rectangle, this time with the diagonal running from top right to bottom left. Pin, then stitch on the marked diagonal, trim, flip back and press. Make four identical units.

3. Lay the units out with the corner squares to form the star block. Join one 2½" x 4½" (6.4 x 11.4cm) stitch-and-flip unit to the bottom of a 4½" (11.4cm) corner square. Press the seam allowances towards the corner square.

4. Stitch a 2½" x 6½" (6.4 x 16.5cm) stitch-and-flip unit to the adjacent side of the corner square. Press the seam allowance towards the 6½" (16.5cm) stitch-and-flip unit. Make four units alike.

5. Stitch the four units together in two rows of two, then join the rows. Press the seam allowances in opposite directions to reduce bulk.

The Chain Star variation swaps the four 4½" (11.4cm) corner squares for four-patch units made from two 2½" (6.4cm) squares of pale grey and two 2½" (6.4cm) squares of charcoal. Make four of these four-patch units per block.

SUGGESTED LAYOUT

My virtual quilt uses twelve Simple Star blocks and thirteen Chain Star variation blocks in five rows of five. The blocks are separated by 2" (5.1cm) wide finished sashing in pale grey with 2" (5.1cm) charcoal grey cornerstones. A 2" (5.1cm) wide mitred border of grey-and-brown striped fabric brings the quilt up to 72" (182.8cm) square, ideal for a throw or bed topper.

71 BLACKFORD'S BEAUTY

This is a wonderfully traditional block and is very straightforward to piece, despite those tricky-looking parallelograms! Using the stitch and flip method (see page 20) makes this much easier! A classic combination of blue, rusty reds and creams with just a touch of gold makes for a very soothing, rich and homely quilt.

For one block you will need
Finished block size:
18" (45.7cm) square

For the corner units
■ Sixteen rusty red 2" (5.1cm) squares
■ Assorted cream prints in the following quantities and sizes: eight 2" (5.1cm) squares, eight 2" x 5" (5.1 x 12.7cm) rectangles, eight 2" x 3½" (5.1 x 8.9cm) rectangles

For the star point units
■ Eight cream 3½" (8.9cm) squares
■ Eight red 3½" (8.9cm) squares
■ Eight blue 3½" x 6½" (8.9 x 16.5cm) rectangles

For the block centre
■ Two 4" (10.2cm) blue squares cut once on the diagonal to yield four triangles
■ One gold 4¾" (12cm) square

Assembling the block
1. To make the corner units, sew the squares and rectangles together in rows, as shown, then join the rows. Make a total of four units.
2. To make the star point units, mark the diagonal on the back of each cream and red square lightly in pencil. Pin the marked squares to the right side of each blue rectangle, making sure that on four of them the diagonals go down from left to right and on four of them the diagonals go down from right to left. Sew on the drawn line, flip back, press and trim the excess to ¼" (6mm). Sew two opposite units together to make one star point. Make a total of four units.
3. To make the block centre sew two of the blue triangles to opposite sides of the gold centre square. Flip back and press, then join the remaining two triangles to the last two sides.
4. Join the corner units, the star points and the block centre into three rows, then join the rows together.

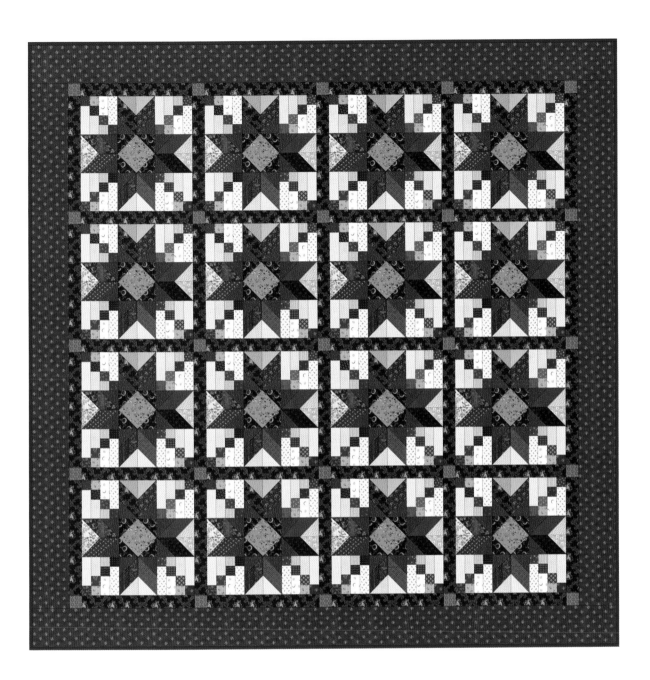

When making multiple different units for a block, it is essential that they all finish to the proper size so that they will fit together without any trouble. Make sure you cut and piece accurately throughout to ensure a perfect fit.

SUGGESTED LAYOUT

For my virtual quilt I have joined sixteen Blackford's Beauty blocks together with 2" (5.1cm) finished sashing in navy blue print and 2" (5.1cm) finished cornerstones in gold. There is a 2" (5.1cm) sashed border and then a final wide border in rusty red that finishes at 6" (15.2cm). The quilt is 94" x 94" (238.8 x 238.8cm).

SQUARE THE CIRCLE

I've dug deep into my virtual stash and used every print I could find that features circles or dots. Using fabrics with a similar theme is a great way to give your quilt a cohesive look, even when the colours are very different.

For one block you will need

Finished block size: 17" (43cm) square

- Twelve 3½" (8.9cm) squares of assorted bright scraps
- One 7½" (19cm) square of assorted bright scraps
- Two 1½" x 7½" (3.8 x 19cm) white solid rectangles
- Eight 1½" x 3½" (3.8 x 8.9cm) white solid rectangles
- Four 1½" x 15½" (3.8 x 39.4cm) white solid rectangles
- Two 1½" x 17½" (3.8 x 44.5cm) white solid rectangles

Assembling the block

1. Take two assorted 3½" (8.9cm) squares and sew one to each side of a 1½" x 3½" (3.8 x 8.9cm) rectangle of white solid. Make two. Press all the seam allowances towards the assorted print fabrics.
2. Sew a 1½" x 7½" (3.8 x 19cm) rectangle of white solid to one side of each of the units you have just made.
3. Sew the white side of the resulting units to each side of the 7½" (19cm) square of bright fabric.
4. Sew a 1½" x 15½" (3.8 x 39.4cm) rectangle of white solid to the top and bottom of this unit.
5. Join four assorted 3½" (8.9cm) squares with three white 1½" x 3½" (3.8 x 8.9cm) strips in a line. Make two.
6. Join these units to the top and bottom of the unit completed in step 4.
7. Sew a 1½" x 15½" (3.8 x 39.4cm) rectangle of white solid to the sides of this unit.
8. Finally join the 1½" x 17½" (3.8 x 44.5cm) white rectangles to the top and bottom of the block.

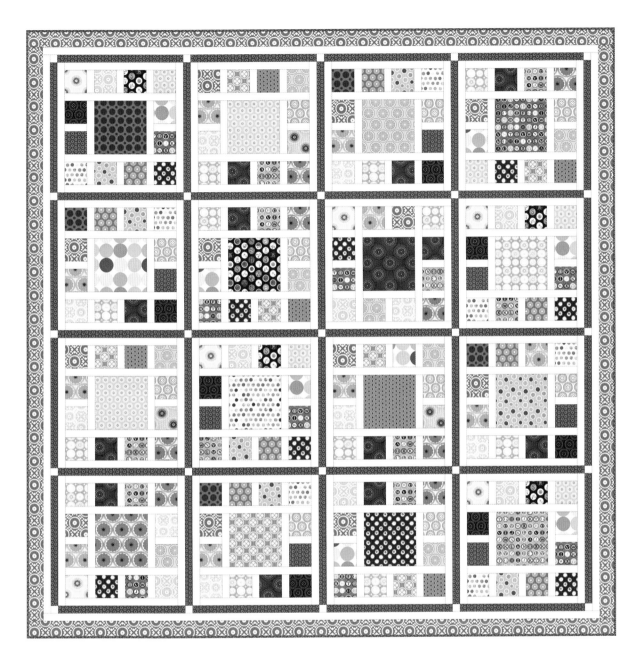

An edge-to-edge quilting pattern featuring swirls of circular motifs would complement this design really well. If you prefer, you could use a walking foot to stitch just inside both edges of every white strip.

SUGGESTED LAYOUT

My virtual quilt uses sixteen Square the Circle blocks, separated by sashing in a deep plum print 1" x 17" (2.5 x 43.2cm) finished and 1" (2.5cm) cornerstones in white solid. I've added a 1" (2.5cm) finished border in a white solid and a 2" (5.1cm) finished border in a red print. The quilt is finished with a deep plum binding. The finished size is 79" x 79" (200.6 x 200.6cm).

TIC TAC TOE

I am often asked for the 'rules' of successful scrap quilting. I think you know what I'm going to say... there are no rules! That said, there are practices that can help to ensure our quilt has the look we want. One is value (the contrast between light and dark fabrics), the other is scale. Scale can be interpreted in many ways, but in this quilt it is about the size of those finished patches, which are just 1" (22.5cm) square.

For one block you will need
Finished block size: 11" (28cm) square
- Thirteen assorted dark print fabric scraps
- White solid or tone on tone

Assembling the block

1. From each of nine dark prints, cut five 1½" (3.8cm) squares (a total of forty-five squares). From the remaining four scraps cut a total of four 1½" (3.8cm) squares.

2. From white solid or tone on tone cut thirty-six 1½" (3.8cm) squares and twelve rectangles each 1½" x 3½" (3.8 x 8.9cm).

3. Join five matching dark and four white 1½" (3.8cm) squares into rows and then join the rows to make a nine-patch block that measure 3½" x 3½" (8.9 x 8.9cm), raw edge to raw edge. Press seam allowances in opposite directions as you go.

4. Make a total of nine of these little nine-patch blocks.

5. Lay the nine-patch blocks out in three rows of three, with the white 1½" x 3½" (3.8 x 8.9cm) rectangles and the remaining four 1½" (3.8cm) dark print squares separating them. Join the blocks and sashing into rows and then join the rows together to make one Tic Tac Toe block.

You could easily strip piece this block, which would make the construction faster. Cut 1½" (3.8cm) strips (instead of squares), sew them together, then cut apart at 1½" (3.8cm) segments.

SUGGESTED LAYOUT

My virtual quilt uses a wide variety of scraps in various prints – blues, greens, purples and pink – with a unifying white tone on tone. Sixteen blocks, separated by 3" (7.6cm) wide finished white sashing and more 3" (7.6cm) finished nine patches, a 1" (2.5cm) finished border 1 and a 5" (12.7cm) finished border 2 brings the quilt up to 71" (180.3cm) square. This is a very simple quilt to enlarge or reduce. Simply add or subtract blocks.

SCRAPPY LATTICE

With the advent and popularity of jelly rolls, most of us have quite a few 2½" (6.4cm) strips and square scraps lurking in our stashes. This quilt uses these small scraps to great effect. I've taken two very simple blocks and combined them to make a quilt that is definitely more than the sum of its parts! I love combining two or more simple blocks. The possibilities are almost endless and watching the secondary patterns emerge is sometimes pretty close to magic.

For one Scrappy Sixteen Patch block you will need
Finished block size: 8" (20.3cm) square
- Sixteen 2½" (6.4cm) squares in various bright print fabrics

Assembling the Scrappy Sixteen Patch block

1. Sew the 2½" (6.4cm) squares together in four rows of four. If you have lots of 2½" (6.4cm) strip scraps, you might consider strip piecing four such strips, and then cross cutting them into 2½" (6.4cm) segments to speed up the construction.

For one Kiss block you will need
Finished block size: 8" (20.3cm) square
- One 4½" (11.4cm) square of solid white fabric
- Eight 2½" (6.4cm) squares in various bright print fabrics

Assembling the Kiss block

1. This uses one of my favourite quick piecing techniques, stitch and flip (see page 20). Take a 4½" (11.4cm) square of white fabric. Mark the diagonal on the back of one bright 2½" (6.4cm) square lightly in pencil and pin it to one corner of the white square. Sew on the diagonal, trim the seam allowance back to ¼" (6mm) and press the bright triangle back.
2. Repeat with a different bright 2½" (6.4cm) square on the opposite corner. Four of these snowball units stitched together make one Kiss block.

SUGGESTED LAYOUT

Thirty-two Kiss blocks and thirty-one Scrappy Sixteen Patch blocks are required for the centre of my virtual quilt, set alternately in seven rows of nine. The quilt centre measures 56" x 72" (142.2 x 182.8cm). To complete the pattern I added partial Kiss blocks to the outer Scrappy Sixteen Patch blocks by 'snowballing' a 4½" x 2½" (11.4 x 6.4cm) white rectangle with an assorted bright 2½" (6.4cm) square. To finish each Scrappy Sixteen Patch you need two of these partial Kiss blocks, 'snowballed' on opposite sides. To finish off the outer Kiss blocks I added four 2½" (6.4cm) squares stitched end to end. I then added border 1 which finishes at 2" (5.1cm), border 2 which finishes at 4" (10.2cm) and border 3 which again finishes at 2" (5.1cm). The finished quilt measures 76" x 92" (193 x 233.7).

LINDEN TREES

On a picnic by the river I saw a group of linden or lime trees and they inspired this quilt's colour scheme. It's a fresh and modern-looking quilt based on a very traditional block and would look great in an assortment of medium/dark scraps of every hue on a cream or tan background.

For one block you will need

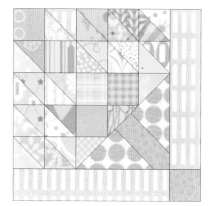

Finished block size:
12" (30.5cm) square
- One light grey 2½" (6.4cm) square
- Seven light grey 2⅞" (7.3cm) squares, cut on one diagonal to yield fourteen triangles
- One light grey 6⅞" (17.5cm) square, cut on one diagonal to yield two triangles (you will need only one per block, one is spare)
- Two light grey 2½" x 10½" (6.4 x 26.7cm) rectangles
- One mid green 1½" x 5" (3.8 x 12.7cm) rectangle, for the tree trunk
- One mid green 2½" (6.4cm) square
- Nine lime/yellow green 2⅞" (7.3cm) squares, cut on one diagonal to yield a total of eighteen triangles (you will only need seventeen)
- Four lime/yellow green 2½" (6.4cm) squares

Assembling the block

1. Pair one light grey and one lime green half square triangle right sides together and sew along the diagonal. Take care not to stretch the bias edge as you do this. Press the seam allowance towards the green fabric. Make a total of fourteen half square triangle units in this manner.
2. Take the 1½" x 5" (3.8 x 12.7cm) strip of mid green fabric for the trunk. Carefully press a ¼" (6mm) turn-under allowance along both long edges.
3. Take the large light grey half square triangle and fold it lightly in half. Using the centre crease as a placement guide, appliqué the prepared trunk strip onto the triangle, by hand or machine (see page 24). The short ends should overhang the triangle. When the appliqué is completed, trim the excess 'trunk' off, so that it is even with the triangle.
4. Lay out the 2½" (6.4cm) squares and half square triangle units, using the block diagram as a guide. Sew the units into rows and then join the rows. Finally, sew the trunk unit to the bottom right corner.
5. Join one mid grey sashing rectangle to the right side. Join the mid green 2½" (6.4cm) square to the last sashing rectangle and press seams towards the sashing. Join the last sashing unit to the bottom of the block.

Use a trip to the countryside, a beautiful garden or the coast to inspire your next scrap quilt's colour scheme. Photographs or postcards can help to capture the moment.

SUGGESTED LAYOUT

My virtual quilt uses a total of thirteen Linden Tree blocks in a diagonal set. The setting triangles were cut from 18¼" (46.4cm) squares, cut on both diagonals to yield four setting triangles. The corner setting triangles were cut from 9½" (24.1cm) squares, and were cut once on the diagonal to yield two corner triangles. A 1" (2.5cm) finished border frames the quilt beautifully. The finished quilt is approximately 53" x 53" (134.6 x 134.6cm) and would make a fabulous throw, wall quilt or picnic blanket.

PINK LEMONADE

This is a humdinger of a quilt block that uses a whole variety of small and medium-sized triangles to create a quilt that's as fresh and zingy as a glass of homemade raspberry lemonade!

For one block you will need
Finished block size:
12" (30.5cm) square
- Four scraps of various pink prints
- Four scraps of various orange prints
- White solid

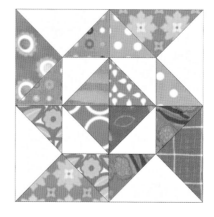

Assembling the block

1. From the pink scraps cut three 3⅞" (9.8cm) squares then cut each one once on the diagonal to yield six triangles. Also cut one 7¼" (18.4cm) square and cut it on both diagonals to yield four triangles (two are spare). Cut the same pieces from the orange scraps.
2. From the white solid cut two 3⅞" (9.8cm) squares, then cut each one once on the diagonal (four triangles). Also cut one 7¼" (18.4cm) square and cut on both diagonals (four triangles).
3. Sew a small half square triangle (HST) unit by joining one small pink and one small white triangle together. Add another two small pink triangles to the white sides of the HST unit to make a right-angled triangle.
4. Join one large pink and one large white triangle along one short edge to make a right-angled triangle, and then sew to the triangle made in step 3 to make a square unit.
5. Repeat steps 3 and 4 to make one more pink and white square and two orange and white squares.
6. Sew the four units together.

Use eight different fabrics instead of four and cut two blocks at a time. This makes the cutting out quicker and makes your blocks even scrappier!

SUGGESTED LAYOUT

For my virtual quilt I have placed twenty Pink Lemonade blocks in a five rows of four, twisting the alternate blocks by a quarter turn. I've added border 1 in solid white at 1" (2.5cm) finished, border 2 in bright pink print which finishes at 4" (10.2cm) and a final white solid border which also finishes at 1" (2.5cm). The whole quilt is 60" x 72" (152.4 x 182.8cm).

Pink Lemonade 177

STAR-SPANGLED BANNER

I couldn't resist a scrappy American flag, perfect for showing your true colours on the fourth of July! Dig into your scrap box, find your cream and tan, red and blue scraps and whip up this quilted flag in time for next year's celebrations!

SUGGESTED LAYOUT

To make my virtual quilt you just need to make one Star-spangled Banner block and then add a 1"/2.5cm finished border of tan fabric. Layer the quilt top with batting (wadding) and backing fabric and quilt as desired. A small all-over quilting design will be sufficient to hold the appliqué stars in place without sewing around every one. Bind with dark red print.

For one block you will need

Finished block size: 40" x 26" (102 x 66cm)

- Three strips of assorted red prints, 2½" x 40½" (6.4 x 102.9cm)
- Four strips of assorted red prints, 2½" x 24½" (6.4 x 62.2cm)
- Three strips of assorted tan/cream prints, 2½" x 40½" 6.4 x 102.9cm)
- Three strips of assorted tan/cream prints, 2½" x 24½" (6.4 x 62.2cm)
- One rectangle of blue print, 14½" x 16½" (36.8 x 42cm)
- Assorted scraps of cream/tan – cut a total of fifty-five point stars from fabric prepared for fusible appliqué (see page 237 for template)

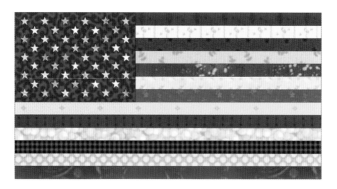

Assembling the block

1. Sew the 40½" (102.9cm) long strips together, alternating the red and cream/tan strips.
2. Sew the 24½" (62.2cm) long strips together, alternating the red and cream/tan strips starting and finishing with a red strip.
3. Sew the shorter strip-pieced panel to the blue rectangle.
4. Sew the blue/red/tan panel to the longer strip-pieced panel.
5. Fuse the 50 stars to the blue panel, using the picture as a guide. See page 24 for appliqué instructions. Sew around the stars if desired.

GOLDFISH BOWL

Bright golden orange fish swim in a pool of azure blue in this fun and playful scrap quilt. A totally different look could be obtained using a different colour scheme... imagine 1930s pastel prints mixed with white solid!

For one block you will need
Finished block size:
18" (45.7cm) square
- Assorted orange scraps
- Assorted blue scraps
- White solid

Assembling the block

1. From the assorted orange scraps, cut four 6⅞" (17.5cm) squares, then cut each one on the diagonal to yield eight triangles (save four for another block). Also cut four 3½" (8.9cm) squares.

2. From the assorted blue scraps, cut eight 3⅞" (9.8cm) squares then cut each one on the diagonal to yield sixteen triangles (save eight for another block).

3. Sew the blue triangles to two adjacent sides of the orange square to make a right-angled triangle then sew the orange triangle to long edge to make a square corner unit. Make four corner units.

4. From the assorted scraps cut eight orange and four blue rectangles, each 1½" x 6½" (3.8 x 16.5cm).

5. Sew two orange and one blue rectangles together, alternating the colours. Make a total of four units.

6. From assorted blue prints cut thirty-six ½" (12mm) squares and from white solid cut thirty-six 1½" (3.8cm) squares.

7. Sew the blue and white squares together in twelve rows of six squares, alternating the colours.

8. Sew three of the rows together as shown. Make four units.

9. Sew the orange/blue units and the checkerboard units together in pairs. Make four. Also cut one 6½" (16.5cm) square in deep blue print.

10. Join the units in rows, then join the rows to complete the block.

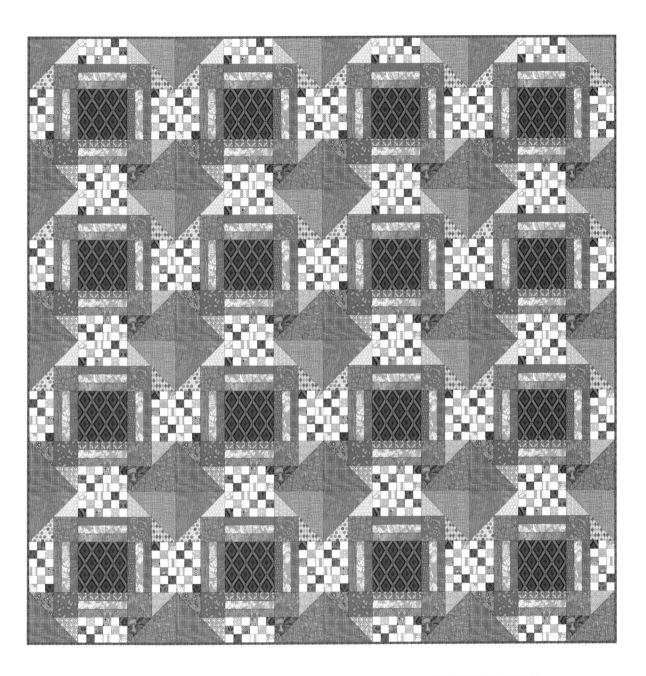

Rather than cut 72 individual squares of white and blue per block, cut three 1½" (3.8cm) strips of white and three 1½" (3.8cm) strips of blue. Sew them together, alternating the colours, and press the seams towards the blue fabrics. Cross cut segments at 1½" (3.8cm) wide. Make several strip-pieced units using different blue fabrics and mix up the cross-cut segments to avoid having two fabrics the same next to each other.

SUGGESTED LAYOUT

For my virtual quilt I have set sixteen blocks together in four rows of four and finished with a blue print binding. The quilt is 72" x 72" (182.8 x 182.8cm).

FALL GRACES

Choose the colours of autumn to make this stunning quilt. I have used solids, but it would look just as wonderful in batiks or prints. Use a variety of background taupes so that you get movement and sparkle across the quilt.

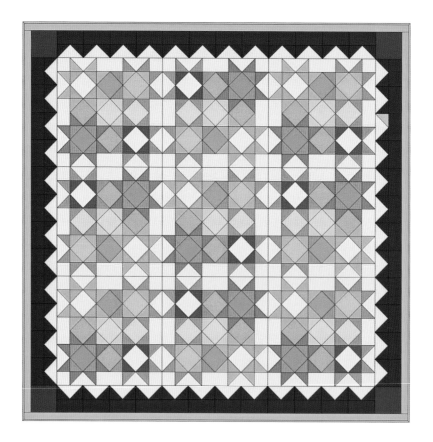

SUGGESTED LAYOUT

For my virtual quilt I have set nine blocks in three rows of three. I have added a 6" (15.2cm) finished border made up of Flying Geese units that are the same size as in the blocks, using taupe for the 'geese' and dark brown for the 'sky'. I have added a 3" x 6" (7.6 x 15.2cm) finished rectangle of dark brown to each flying geese unit. The 6" (15.2cm) cornerstones of this border are cut from mid brown solid. The final 1" (2.5cm) finished border is in bright gold. The quilt finishes at 62" x 62" (157.4 x 157.4cm).

For one block you will need

Finished block size: 16" (40.7cm) square

- Nine different 'fall-coloured' scraps – from four of them cut four 2⅞" (7.3cm) squares, each one cross cut on one diagonal to yield eight triangles (thirty-two in total); from the remaining five cut two 2⅞" (7.3cm) squares, and then cross cut each one on one diagonal to yield four triangles (twenty in total)
- From various taupe scraps cut nine 3⅜" (8.6cm) squares for the star centres, four 2½" (6.4cm) squares, four 2½" x 4½" (6.4 x 11.4cm) rectangles, and two 5¼" (13.3cm) squares cross cut on both diagonals to yield eight triangles

Assembling the block

1. Piece eight Flying Geese units and nine Square-in-a-Square units as shown, placing the colours carefully.
2. Arrange the pieced units and the remaining taupe squares and rectangles to make the block.
3. Join the units, squares and rectangles into rows.
4. Join the rows together.

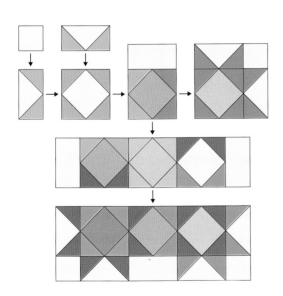

SUPER ECONOMY

The Economy block is a time-served classic when it comes to scrap blocks. I thought I'd rename it Super Economy, as it really is a far more fabulous block than its humble name suggests, particularly when it's pieced in your favourite colours. Here I've combined orange, pink and purple with a favourite black-and-white polka dot.

SUGGESTED LAYOUT

For my virtual quilt I set twenty Super Economy blocks together with 2" (5.1cm) finished sashing in black-and-white random polka dot and 2" (5.1cm) finished solid black cornerstones. The first border in yellow finishes at 1" (2.5cm), the second border in black-and-white polka dot finishes at 4" (10.2cm) and a final 1" (2.5cm) finished border of yellow brings the quilt up to 70" x 84" (177.8 x 213.3cm). It is bound in solid black.

For one block you will need

Finished block size: 12" (30.5cm) square
- One pink print 6½" (16.5) square
- Two purple print 5¼" (13.3cm) squares cut on one diagonal to yield four triangles
- Two orange 7" (17.8cm) squares cut on the diagonal to yield four triangles

Assembling the block

1. Sew two of the purple triangles to opposite sides of the centre pink square. Press the seams towards the purple triangles.
2. Add the remaining two purple triangles to the last two sides of the pink centre square. Press the seams towards the purple fabrics.
3. Add the orange triangles in the same way: sew to opposite corners first, press, then add the last two triangles.

81 SCRAPPY HEARTS

Romantic and unashamedly girly, this quilt strewn with foundation pieced hearts will dent your stash and would make a smashing gift for your true love. If you've never tried paper foundation piecing this, would be a perfect first block.

SUGGESTED LAYOUT

For my virtual quilt I set sixty-four blocks in eight rows of eight, flipping alternate blocks 180 degrees. I then added a 1" (2.5cm) finished border in lilac polka dot, a 3½" (8.9cm) finished border in pink and a final 1" (2.5cm) border in lilac polka dot. The quilt finishes at 59" x 59" (149.8 x 149.8cm).

For one block you will need

Finished block size: 6" (15.2cm) square

- Two scraps of the same pink/red print fabric for the heart
- Very pale pink tone or batik for the block background

Assembling the quilt top

1. Download and print (see page 224 for link) or photocopy one copy of Scrappy Heart foundation A (page 237).

2. Following the general instructions for paper foundation piecing (page 21), piece the block in numerical order, trimming the seam allowances as you go.

3. Press the finished block carefully. Leave the paper intact until all the blocks have been sewn together.

BRIGHT HOPES STAR

This block uses a very clever and remarkably simple partial seam construction method. A very long title for a very simple technique... don't be alarmed, it's easy!

SUGGESTED LAYOUT

For my virtual quilt I have set thirteen Bright Hopes Star blocks on point, separated by 1" (2.5cm) finished sashing, 1" (2.5cm) finished cornerstones in dark purple batik and mid grey solid setting triangles. The large setting triangles are cut from two 18¼" (46.3cm) squares, cut on both diagonals to yield eight setting triangles. The corner setting triangles are cut from two 9½" (24.1cm) squares, cut once on the diagonal to yield four corner triangles. The quilt has a 1" (2.5cm) finished border to match the sashing and a final border of blue damask print which finishes at 3½" (8.9cm) for a quilt that is approximately 56" x 56" (142.2 x 142.2cm).

For one block you will need

Finished block size: 10" (25.4cm) square

- One dark purple batik 2½" (6.4cm) square
- Two lime green print 4⅞" squares cut on one diagonal to yield a total of four triangles
- One mid blue batik 5¼" (13.3cm) square cut on both diagonals to yield four triangles
- One mid grey 5¼" (13.3cm) square solid cut on both diagonals to yield four triangles
- Four rectangles of mid grey solid each 2½" x 4½" (6.4 x 11.4cm)

Assembling the block

1. Sew the mid grey solid and lime green batik triangles together in pairs. Make a total of four units.
2. Sew a large mid blue triangle to each green/grey triangle unit and press the seams towards the green fabric.
3. Sew a mid grey solid rectangle to one side of each pieced triangle unit as shown.
4. Place one pieced triangle unit and the centre dark purple batik square right sides together, lining up the raw edges. Sew 1" (2.5cm) of the seam, backstitch and clip your threads. This is the partial seam. Press the part of the seam that you have sewn towards the pieced triangle unit.
5. Line up the next pieced triangle unit with the next side of the centre square, adjacent to the side with the partial seam. Sew the entire seam this time.
6. Continue to work around the centre square until you have added the fourth and final pieced triangle unit.
7. Sew the remaining 1½" (3.8cm) of the first partial seam.

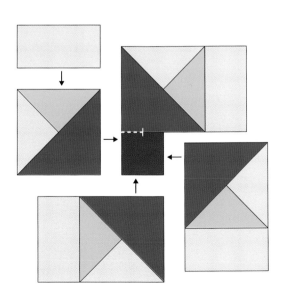

If you are cutting your sashing strips on the bias, as I have, to make the most of a striped fabric, you will need to starch your fabric heavily before you cut it to prevent distortion. Spray the fabric lightly, iron dry, then repeat two or three more times until the fabric is very firm and crisp.

83 GEESE MEET

I love Flying Geese units. They are one of those fundamentals in quilting that never fails and can look as modern or as traditional as you like. Fabric choices make all the difference and here I've gone for a contemporary take on tradition, using a variety of black, coral, blue and green prints.

SUGGESTED LAYOUT

For my virtual quilt I have sewn sixteen Geese Meet blocks together in four rows of four and added border 1 to finish at 1" (2.5cm) and border 2 to finish at 2" (5.1cm). The whole quilt measures 38" x 38" (95.5 x 95.5cm), making a perfect table topper or small wall quilt.

For one block you will need

Finished block size: 8" (20.3cm)
- Scraps of assorted black, coral, blue and green prints
- A good variety of tan and cream prints

Assembling the block

1. Download and print (see page 224 for link) or photocopy four copies of Geese Meet foundation A (page 237).
2. Following the general instructions for paper foundation piecing (page 21), piece the foundation units in numerical order, taking careful note of colour placement and trimming the seam allowances as you go.
3. Trim the units to 4½" (11.4cm).
4. Join the four units using the diagram to help you. Leave the paper intact until all the blocks have been sewn together.

84 STRIP SCRAP QUILT

Sometimes we all need to make a quilt in a hurry – an unexpected baby shower gift, perhaps, or a lap quilt to show a sick friend that we care. This quilt is so fast to make it that can be done in a day! Get the coffee on, grab your leftover 2½" (6.4cm) strips and let's quilt!

SUGGESTED LAYOUT

To finish this quilt, all you need to do is layer it with batting (wadding) and backing fabric cut 2" (5.1cm) bigger on all sides. I would suggest quilting this very quickly, using a walking foot and 'wobbly' lines running vertically down the quilt every ¾" (19mm) or so. Just use the first line as a guide and line up the edge of your walking foot with it.

You will need
Finished quilt size: 40" x 35" (102 x 89cm)

- Twenty jelly roll-type strips, for example 2½" x 42" (6.4 x 106.7cm) – use leftovers from another jelly roll quilt, leftover binding strips or cut your own from your stash
- Two 2½" x 42" (6.4cm x 106.7cm) strips of a bright solid – I have used yellow

Assembling the quilt top

1. Sew all of your jelly roll strips together to make a panel that measures approximately 40½" x 42" (102.9 x 106.7cm).
2. Trim one edge straight, then cut three segments to the following measurements: 40½" x 8½" (102.9 x 21.6cm), 40½" x 16½" (102.9 x 42cm) and 40½" x 8½" (102.9 x 21.6cm). You will have a little of the strip-pieced panel left over, which would be great to make a coordinating pillow!
3. Flip the 8½" (21.6cm) panels through 180 degrees and sew each one to a bright solid strip.
4. Sew the 16½" (42cm) panel in the centre.

85 SCRAP STARS

Such a simple block as this pops up many times in quilt designs, usually as part of a larger block. On its own it creates a wonderful 'skewed star' and would certainly make a dent in anyone's scrap pile! It uses the stitch and flip method (see page 20), which makes construction as easy as 1, 2, 3!

SUGGESTED LAYOUT

For my virtual quilt I have set 180 blocks in a twelve rows of fifteen arrangement then added a 3" (7.6cm) finished border in red/tan print and a 1" (2.5cm) finished outer border in dark red print. The quilt measures 56" x 68" (142.2 x 172.7cm).

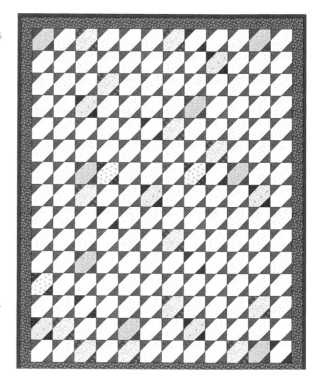

Use a propelling pencil to mark lines when using the stitch and flip method. This will ensure that your pencil line is always very fine and accurate, essential for perfect blocks!

For one block you will need

Finished block size: 4" (10.2cm)
- One 4½" (11.4cm) square of cream/white with red print
- Two 2½" (6.4cm) squares of assorted red prints

Assembling the block

1. Draw the diagonal lightly in pencil on the back of both red squares, then pin them to opposite corners of the cream/white square, right sides together. Ensure that the pencil lines go across the corners!
2. Sew along the lines. Cut the corners away, leaving a ¼" (6mm) seam allowance, and then press back.

SQUARES FRAMED

Easy peasy doesn't have to mean boring! A simple checkerboard is lifted with bright white frames. The key to making a monochromatic colour scheme exciting is to use every shade you can find – here, aquas, teals, turquoise and sky blue sit with ocean blue, navy and blues verging into purple. I've said it before and I'll say it again – 'more is more'!

You will need

Quilt size: 60" (150cm) square

- 312 solid white 2½" (6.4cm) squares
- 312 assorted teal/blue and navy 2½" (6.4cm) squares
- White fabric for the frames cut into 2½" (6.4cm) wide strips

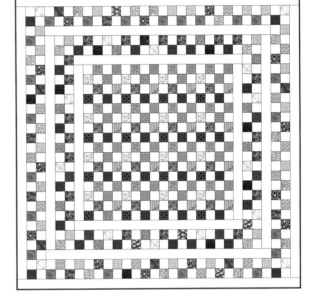

Assembling the quilt top

1. The centre checkerboard contains 256 squares. That's 128 blue and 128 white sewn together in a 16 x 16 arrangement.
2. Add your first white border with two strips cut to 32½" (82.5cm) and two strips cut to 36½" (92.7cm).
3. The second frame of blue and white squares is made up of 80 white and 80 blue squares. I find it easiest to sew them into four-patch units, then sew the four-patch units together.
4. The second white border needs two strips cut to 44½" (113cm) and two strips cut to 48½" (123cm).
5. The last frame of blue and white squares is made up of 104 white squares and 104 blue squares, again sewn into four-patch units first and then sewn together.
6. The third and final white frame uses two strips cut to 56½" (143.5cm) and two strips cut to 60½" (153.7cm).
7. The quilt is bound with deep blue batik.

When I have to cut this many of a single shape, I am so very grateful for my die cutting machine. Die cutting produces perfect results every time and it's the easiest and fastest way I've discovered to cut out my quilts (see page 15).

87 MODERN AMISH SAMPLER QUILT

It's incredible how eight simple shapes can combine to create almost endless variation! This sampler quilt illustrates that principle and although only the centre block is patterned you can use any 12" (30.5cm) finished blocks in place of my selection. I have used my die cutter to make the cutting and construction super fast and super easy, but you can use traditional rotary cutting instructions if you prefer!

For one Modern Amish Star block you will need:

Finished block size: 24" (61cm) square

- Four leaf green 3½" (8.9cm) squares
- Two light green 3⅞" (9.8cm) squares cut on one diagonal to yield four triangles
- Eight mustard 3½" (8.9cm) squares
- One mustard 4¾" (12cm) square
- Four red 6⅞" (17.5cm) squares cut on one diagonal to yield eight triangles
- Four pink 3⅞" (9.8cm) squares cut on one diagonal to yield eight triangles
- Six black 3⅞" (9.8cm) squares cut on one diagonal to yield twelve triangles
- Three black 7¼" (18.4cm) squares cut on both diagonals to yield twelve triangles

- Four purple 3⅞" (9.8cm) squares cut on one diagonal to yield eight triangles
- Two light aqua 3⅞" (9.8cm) squares cut on one diagonal to yield four triangles
- Four bright blue 3⅞" (9.8cm) squares cut on one diagonal to yield eight triangles
- Two light green 3⅞" (9.8cm) squares cut on one diagonal to yield four triangles

SUGGESTED LAYOUT

For my Modern Amish Sampler I have sewn a total of thirty-two 12" (30.5cm) blocks and joined them with 2" (5.1cm) finished sashing in black. I have added a 2" (5.1cm) finished border in black, then a 1" (2.5cm) finished border in pale aqua. The Flying Geese border uses one 7¼" (18.4cm) bright solid scrap and four 3⅞" (9.8cm) black squares to make four Flying Geese units using the no-waste method (see page 20). You will need a total of 112 Flying Geese units (cut from twenty-eight 7¼"/18.4cm bright squares and one hundred and twelve 3⅞"/9.8cm black squares) for the 6" (15.2cm) finished border. I have then added a 1" (2.5cm) finished border in pale aqua, a 1" (2.5cm) finished border in green and a final 2" (5.1cm) finished border in black solid. The quilt finishes at 108" x 108" (274.3 x 274.3cm).

MODERN AMISH SAMPLER QUILT

Assembling the block

1. Start by piecing the centre star. Use the 4¾" (12cm) mustard square and the four light aqua triangles to sew a square on point unit.
2. Use four of the black 7¼" (18.4cm) triangles and the bright blue 3⅞" (9.8cm) triangles to make four Flying Geese units.
3. Finally use four of the purple triangles and the smaller black triangles to make four half square triangle units. Sew the units together to make the centre star.
4. Make the corner units by sewing the light green triangles and the remaining purple triangles together to make half square triangle (HST) units. Sew one of these units to a mustard 3½" (8.9cm) square.
5. Sew a leaf green and a mustard 3½" (8.9cm) square together and sew this to the unit made in step 4. Make four such units.
6. Make a Flying Geese unit using two bright pink triangles and one large black triangle. Sew two more 3⅞" (9.8cm) black triangles to the sides of the flying geese unit and then sew a large black triangle to the base. Finally sew a large red triangle to each of two sides of the unit. Make four such units.
7. Sew the units together in rows and then sew the rows together.

The Amish Star has pale aqua sashing sewn around it. The sashing pieces are cut as follows: two at 1½" x 24½" (3.8 x 62.2cm) and two at 1½" x 26½" (3.8 x 67.3cm).

CHRISTMAS STARS

I love it when I can include some kind of sashing or frame around a patchwork block – it makes putting the quilt together so much faster! I've coloured this quilt for a very traditional Christmas at the cabin, but it would look equally good in whatever scraps you happen to have.

For one block you will need

Finished block size: 9" (22.9cm) square

- Ten 2" (5.1cm) squares of assorted red prints
- Ten 2" (5.1cm) squares of assorted green prints
- Four 2" (5.1cm) squares of cream print
- One 4¼" (8.9cm) square of cream print
- One 3½" (8.9cm) square of gold print
- Four 2⅜" (6cm) squares of gold print

Assembling the block

1. Sew two red and two green squares together, alternating the colours. Make two units.
2. Sew three red and three green squares together, alternating the colours. Make two units.
3. Use the no-waste Flying Geese method (see page 20) to make four Flying Geese units using the four gold 2⅜" (6cm) squares and the 4¼" (8.9cm) square of cream print.
4. Make the centre star block by sewing a Flying Geese unit to two opposite sides of the 3½" (8.9cm) gold square. Sew a cream print square to each end of the remaining Flying Geese units. Make two, then sew them to the remaining sides of the centre square.
5. Sew a row of four green/red squares to the top of the star and four red/green squares to the bottom. Add the rows of six squares to the sides, being careful to alternate the colours.

SUGGESTED LAYOUT

For my virtual quilt I have set thirteen Christmas Stars blocks on point and made pieced setting triangles from a 5" (12.7cm) square of red fabric and two triangles of green fabric made by cutting a 7⅝" (19.4cm) square on both diagonals to yield four triangles (two will be spare). The corner setting triangles are made by cutting a 7⅜" (18.7cm) square and then cutting it in half on one diagonal to yield two triangles. Border 1 finishes at 1½" (3.8cm), border 2 finishes at 3" (7.6cm) and border 3 at 1½" (3.8cm). The finished quilt measures just over 50½" x 50½" (128.2 x 128.2cm).

89 STAR IN THE CABIN

Who doesn't love a Log Cabin block? There are many versions and this one is lit up with a galaxy of stars! This design manages to be both modern and timeless and would work in any selection of favourite prints or solids. Just make sure that there is good contrast between both 'log' fabrics and whatever you choose for your stars. This is a complex block to piece that will have friends wondering: how did you do that?

For one block you will need

Finished block size:
12" (30.5cm) square

- Assorted scraps of light grey prints and batiks, each 1½" (3.8cm) wide and between 5½" (14cm) and 8½" (21.6cm) long. You will also need some 1½" (3.8cm) squares
- Assorted scraps of medium/dark purple prints and batiks, each 1½" (3.8cm) wide and between 4½" (11.4cm) and 11½" (29.2cm) long. You will also need some 1½" (3.8cm) squares
- Assorted yellow scraps for the stars (I used two different solids)

Keep your pieces organized in zip-loc bags that contain all the pieces to make one block... this is one quilt that I would recommend you make one block at a time!

SUGGESTED LAYOUT

My virtual quilt consists of sixteen blocks in four rows of four to make a quilt that is 48" x 48" (122 x 122cm).

STAR IN THE CABIN

Assembling the block

1. For the central star you will need one 2½" (6.4cm) yellow square, three 1½" (3.8cm) light grey squares, one 1½" (3.8cm) dark purple square, two light grey/yellow Flying Geese units and two dark purple/yellow Flying Geese units. To make the Flying Geese units, cut a 2½" x 1½" (6.4 x 3.8cm) rectangle of 'goose' fabric and two 1½" (3.8cm) squares of 'sky' fabric. Use the stitch and flip method (see page 20) to create a total of four Flying Geese units.

2. Sew the central star unit, which should measure 4½" (11.4cm) square when pieced.

3. Add the first round of 'logs' as follows: 1½" x 4½" (3.8 x 11.4cm) purple, 1½" x 5½" (3.8 x 14cm) purple, 1½" x 5½" (3.8 x 14cm) grey and 1½" x 5½" (3.8 x 14cm) grey. Align the top of this last log with the top edge of the first (purple) log and start sewing from here. Leave the final 1" (2.5cm) unsewn. This is a partial seam and we will finish it later.

4. Add the second round of logs: 1½" x 6½" (3.8 x 16.5cm) purple, 1½" x 7½" (3.8 x 19cm) purple, 1½" x 6½" (3.8 x 16.5cm) grey and 1½" x 6½" (3.8 x 16.5cm) grey, aligning the last grey log with the top of the block.

5. Add the round three and four logs in the same way. There will be a square hole in the bottom left corner where the second star will be sewn.

6. For the second star unit: make two Flying Geese units with a round four grey goose and yellow 'sky'. Make two round two and two round three grey/yellow half square triangle units by pairing up grey and yellow 1½" (3.8cm) squares, marking and then sewing on the diagonal and trimming ¼" (6mm) away from the centre diagonal. You will also need one 2½" (6.4cm) yellow square for the star centre, one 1½" (3.8cm) round one grey square and three 1½" (3.8cm) round four grey squares.

7. Arrange the patches as shown and sew them together to create the second star.

8. Join the second star to the bottom of the logs on the left-hand side of the block, completing the partial seam on the round one grey log as you do so.

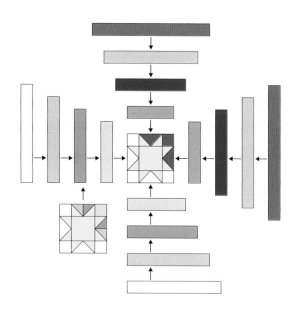

PEONY BLOCK

Appliqué is a fantastic technique for using scraps and is one of my favourites. Use whatever appliqué technique you like best, but remember that appliqué templates never have a seam/turn-under allowance added – so if you want to use turned-edge methods, you will need to add this on.

SUGGESTED LAYOUT

For my virtual quilt I have set sixty-four Peony Blocks together separated by 1" (2.5cm) finished sashing in solid white and 1" (2.5cm) finished cornerstones. I have joined four blocks of similar colour to create a larger block and here the cornerstone is green. In between these larger joined blocks the sashing and cornerstones are white. I've added a number of borders to this quilt: borders 1, 2, 4 and 5 all finish at 1" (2.5cm) and border 3 finishes at 5" (12.7cm). The quilt is 75" x 75" (190.5 x 190.5cm).

For one block you will need

Finished block size: 6" (15.2cm) square
- One 6½" (16.5cm) square of cream or white print for the block background
- Five scraps of various greens for the appliqué stem and leaves
- One 3½" (8.9cm) square of bright fabric for the flower

Assembling the block

1. Use the Peony Block templates (see page 237) to cut one small leaf and one small leaf reversed, one large leaf and one large leaf reversed, one stem and one peony flower. Prepare the shapes for your chosen method of appliqué (see page 21).
2. Gently fold a crease through one diagonal on your background square. Use this crease to help you place the design elements. Make sure that the base of the stem is ¾" (19mm) in from the bottom corner of the background and that the flower is around 1" (2.5cm) in from the top corner.
3. Appliqué the shapes onto the background, sewing the stem first, followed by the leaves and finally the flower.

91 INDIGO PINWHEELS

This is a great quilt for showing off a collection of favourite fabrics: indigo prints as I've used, Dutch chintz, civil war reproductions or vibrant modern prints and solids would all look utterly wonderful!

For one block you will need
Finished block size: 9" (22.9cm) square

- Ten 2⅜" (6cm) squares of assorted indigo blue fabrics
- Ten 2⅜" (6cm) squares of solid white fabric
- Four 3½" (8.9cm) squares of assorted indigo blue fabrics

Assembling the block

1. Draw a diagonal line on the back of each white square with a pencil.
2. Lay one marker white square on top of an indigo 2⅜" (6cm) square, right sides together. Sew a ¼" (6mm) seam either side of the marked line. Cut apart on the marked line and press the two half square triangle (HST) units open. Make a total of twenty HST units. See page 19.
3. Sew four HST units together to make a pinwheel, taking care to alternate the colours. Make a total of five pinwheel units.
4. Using the diagram to guide you, arrange the five pinwheels units and the four indigo blue 3½" (8.9cm) squares together to make the pinwheel block. Sew the units into rows, then sew the rows together.

Keep your first pinwheel unit next to you at the sewing machine as a reminder – all of your pinwheels should be identical to this one!

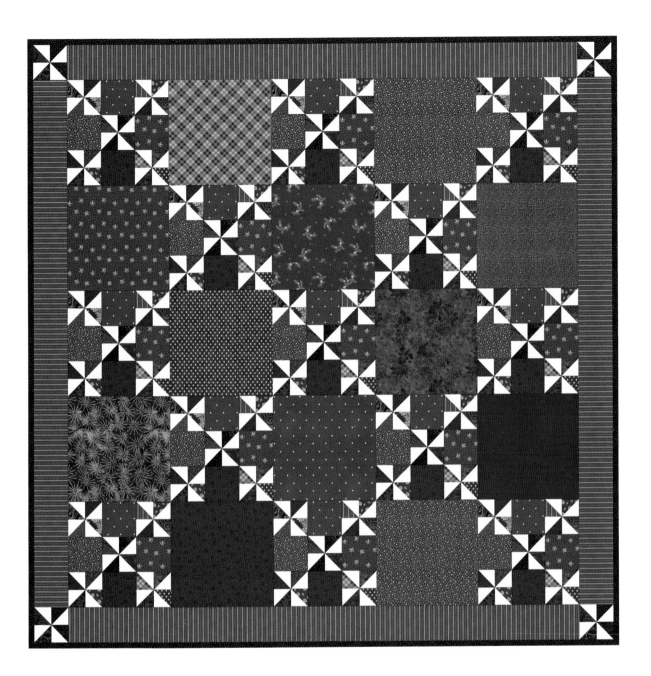

SUGGESTED LAYOUT

For my virtual quilt I have set thirteen Pinwheel blocks together with twelve 9½" (24.1cm) cut squares of indigo fabric in five rows of five. I have added a 3" (7.6cm) finished indigo border with four extra small pinwheel blocks at the corners. The finished quilt is 51" x 51" (129.5 x 129.5cm).

MAZE RUNNER

Flying geese units dart this way and that, trying to escape the maze of blue batiks and sandy pathways.

For one block you will need

Finished block size:
16" (40.7cm) square

- Two strips of blue batik, each 2½" x 16½" (6.4 x 42cm)
- One strip of sand-coloured batik, 4½" x 16½" (11.4 x 42cm)
- Four assorted print 5¼" (13.3cm) squares in various shades of pink, moss green, blue and rust
- Sixteen pale cream batik 2⅞" (7.3cm) squares

Assembling the block

1. Mark the diagonal on the wrong side of each cream batik 2⅞" (7.3cm) square using a pencil.
2. Use the no-waste method (see page 20) to make a total of sixteen Flying Geese units, using the marked cream squares for the 'sky' and the assorted pink, moss green, blue and rust squares as the 'geese'.
3. Sew eight of the Flying Geese units together into a row 4½" x 16½" (11.4 x 42cm). Make two units.
4. Sew the rows of flying geese together with the blue and sand-coloured batik strips, as shown.

Make four blocks at a time, using sixteen assorted 5¼" (13.3cm) squares of pink/green/blue and rust squares to make a wider variety of Flying Geese units. Mix the fabrics up throughout the four blocks. Making your blocks in batches of four will help to distribute your scraps more evenly and the piecing goes by much quicker!

SUGGESTED LAYOUT

For my virtual quilt I have set sixteen blocks together in four rows of four, twisting alternate blocks by 90 degrees. I have added a Flying Geese border that finishes at 4" (10.2cm), using the same sized units as in the main quilt block. You will need to make an additional one hundred and twenty-eight Flying Geese units (using thirty-two 5¼"/13.3cm squares of 'geese' fabric and one hundred and twenty-eight 2⅞" squares of cream fabric for the 'sky'). The border has 4" (10.2cm) finished cornerstones in the same bright blue batik as the blocks. The final plain border finishes at 2" (5.1cm) and the quilt measures 76" x 76" (193 x 193cm).

PATRIOT CHAIN

Red, blue and tan... a wonderfully strong colour combination and an equally strong design. I love the combination of stars and chains in a quilt and the pieced sashing gives the blocks just a little extra room to breathe.

SUGGESTED LAYOUT

For my quilt I have arranged twelve Patriot Star blocks with thirteen Patriot Chain blocks in five rows of five. I have separated the blocks with 2" (5.1cm) finished pieced sashing. To make the sashing, sew a red print 2½" (6.4cm) square to each end of a 12½" x 2½" (31.7 x 6.4cm) rectangle of tan print. The cornerstones are cut at 2½" (6.4cm) from assorted dark blue prints. The quilt is 92" x 92" (233.7 x 233.7cm) and is finished with a dark blue binding.

For one Patriot Star block you will need

Finished block size: 16" (40.7cm) square

- Four 4½" (11.4cm) squares of dark blue 1
- Four 2⅞" (7.3cm) squares of dark blue 2
- One 5¼" (13.3cm) square of dark blue 2
- Ten 2½" (6.4cm) squares of medium blue
- Twelve 2⅞" (7.3cm) squares of medium/dark red print
- Two 5¼" (13.3cm) squares of tan print
- Eight 2½" (6.4cm) squares of tan print
- Four 2⅞" (7.3cm) squares of light tan print

Note: I've referred to dark blues 1 and 2 in the instructions to make the pattern easier to understand, but you could use the same blue throughout if you prefer.

Assembling the Patriot Star block

1. Start by making the corner units, using the stitch and flip method (see page 20). Take one blue 4½" (11.4cm) square and two 2½" (6.4cm) squares of tan print. Mark the diagonal on the back of both tan squares, then pin them to opposite corners of the blue square. Sew along the lines, then trim the excess to ¼". (6mm). Flip the tan square back and press. Make a total of four corner units.

2. Using four of the red and the light tan 2⅞" (7.3cm) squares, make a total of eight half square triangle (HST) units (see page 19).

3. Use the remaining red squares to make Flying Geese units. Pair four red squares with the 5¼" (13.3cm) square of blue and four red squares with the 5¼" (13.3cm) square of tan and use the no-waste method (see page 20).

4. Pair the dark blue 2⅞" (7.3cm) squares with the remaining 5¼" (13.3cm) tan squares and make four more Flying Geese units.

5. Arrange the Flying Geese units, half square triangle units, medium blue squares and the red centre square, using the diagram as a guide.

6. Sew the units into rows, then sew the rows together.

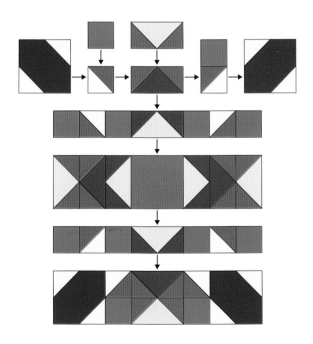

93

PATRIOT CHAIN

For one Patriot Chain block you will need

Finished block size: 16" (40.7cm) square

- Twelve 2½" (6.4cm) squares of assorted dark blue prints
- Sixteen 2½" (6.4cm) squares of assorted red prints
- Four 2½" x 4½" (6.4 x 11.4cm) rectangles of assorted red prints
- Four 2½" x 4½" (6.4 x 11.4cm) rectangles of assorted tan prints
- Four 2½" x 8½" (6.4 x 21.6cm) rectangles of assorted tan prints
- One 4½" (11.4cm) square of dark blue print

Assembling the Patriot Chain block

1. Sew two red and two blue 2½" (6.4cm) squares together to make a four patch. Make four units.
2. Sew a red 2½" (6.4cm) square to each end of a 2½" x 4½" (6.4 x 11.4cm) tan rectangle. Make four units.
3. Sew a red 2½" x 4½" (6.4 x 11.4cm) rectangle to two opposite sides of the 4½" (11.4cm) centre blue square. Sew a blue 2½" (6.4cm) square to each end of the remaining 2½" x 4½" (6.4 x 11.4cm) red rectangles, then sew these units to the last two sides of the centre square.
4. Sew a red 2½" (6.4cm) square to each end of each of the 2½" x 4½" (6.4cm) tan rectangles, then sew a tan 8½" (21.6cm) rectangle to this unit. Make a total of four units.
5. Sew the units together as shown.

Make a test block before you start cutting the pieces for a whole quilt. It will help you learn the construction method and also give you a chance to see if you like your colour choices!

94

COLOURICIOUS

I've named this block and quilt in honour of my friend Jamie. I have stuck to quite classic colour wheel pairings of complimentary colours but as the song quite rightly says 'anything goes'!

For one block A you will need
Finished block size: 10" (25.4cm)
- One 2½" (6.4cm) square of blue for the block centre
- Four rectangles of orange cut at 1½" (3.8cm) wide – cut two rectangles at 2½" (6.4cm) and two rectangles at 4½" (11.4cm)
- Four rectangles of purple cut at 2½" (6.4cm) wide – cut two rectangles at 4½" (11.4cm) and two rectangles at 8½" (21.6cm)
- Four rectangles of leaf green cut at 1½" (3.8cm) wide – cut two rectangles at 8½" (21.6cm) and two rectangles at 10½" (26.7cm)

For one block B you will need
Finished block size:
10" (25.4cm) square
- Various scraps in shades of gold and yellow, teal, red, pink and green

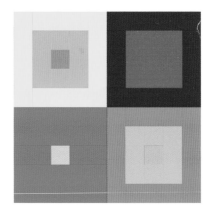

Assembling block A
1. Start with the centre square and sew the 2½" (6.4cm) rectangles of orange to opposite sides. Press the seams towards the orange fabric, then sew the 4½" (11.4cm) rectangles to the remaining two sides. Press as before.
2. Continue to add the purple strips and then the leaf green rectangles.

Assembling block B
1. The top left and bottom right quarters are the same: a 1½" (3.8cm) centre square surrounded by two 1½" (3.8cm) squares and two 1½" x 3½" (3.8 x 8.9cm) rectangles and then two 1½" x 3½" (3.8 x 8.9cm) rectangles and two 1½" x 5½" (3.8 x 14cm) rectangles.
2. Top right quarter: a 3½" (8.9cm) centre square surrounded by a 1½" (3.8cm) border consisting of: two 1½" x 3½" (3.8 x 8.9cm) and two 1½" x 5½" (3.8 x 14cm) rectangles.
3. Bottom left quarter: a 1½" (3.8cm) centre square surrounded by two 1½" x 2½" (3.8 x 6.4cm) and two 2½" x 5½" (6.4 x 14cm) rectangles.
4. Sew the four quarters together.

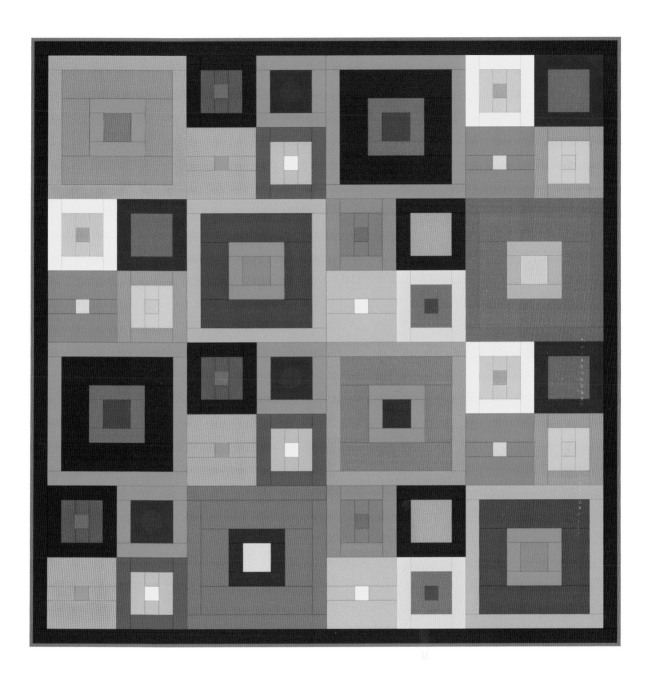

SUGGESTED LAYOUT

This design consists of two blocks, A and B. For my virtual quilt I have set eight of block A and eight of block B together in four rows of four. There is a final border of deep purple solid, which finishes at 1" (2.5cm), and the quilt is bound in bright orange. The finished quilt is 42" x 42" (106.7 x 106.7cm).

CHRISTMAS CROWN

Another lovely traditional pairing of red, gold and green mixed with a plaid for a cosy country Christmas. There are a lot of small pieces to cut, so try to be organized. Rest assured – this block will use up all your tiny scraps!

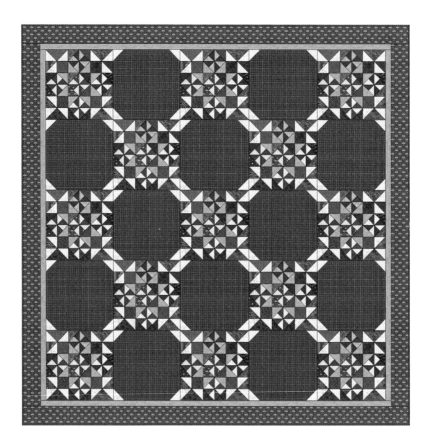

SUGGESTED LAYOUT

For my virtual quilt I have I have set thirteen Christmas Crown blocks together with plaid alternate blocks. I have 'snowballed' the corners of the plaid blocks by laying a 2½" (6.4cm) cream square, right sides together, on the corner, with the diagonal marked lightly in pencil, and sewing on the marked diagonal line. The excess is then trimmed away, leaving a ¼" (6mm) seam allowance. This is repeated on all four corners. I've added a 1" (2.5cm) finished border in yellow/gold and a 3" (7.6cm) finished border in a green/gold print. The quilt finishes at 68" x 68" (172.7 x 172.7cm).

For one block you will need

Finished block size: 12" (30.5cm) square

- Eight green 2⅞" (7.3cm) squares, cut on one diagonal to yield sixteen medium triangles
- One 5¼" (13.3cm) green square, cut on both diagonals to yield four large triangles
- Four green 2½" (6.4cm) squares
- Six 2⅞" (7.3cm) cream squares, cut on one diagonal to yield twelve medium triangles
- Five cream 3¼" (8.3cm) squares, cut on both diagonals to yield twenty small triangles
- Five red 4¼" (10.8cm) squares, cut on both diagonals to yield twenty small triangles
- Four yellow/gold 2⅞" (7.3cm) squares, cut on one diagonal to yield eight medium triangles

Assembling the block

1. Start by piecing the red and cream pinwheel units, which are made using the red and cream small triangles.
2. Add four medium green triangles to one pinwheel for the block centre and then join two green and two yellow/gold medium triangles to the remaining four pinwheel units for the middle units. Be very careful to follow the block diagram for colour placement.
3. Join two medium cream triangles to each side of a large green triangle to create a Flying Geese unit. Make four units in total.
4. Join one more medium cream and medium green triangle to make a half square triangle. Sew this to a 2½" (6.4cm) green square, then finally join this unit to the Flying Geese as shown. Make four units in total.
5. Sew the units together into rows, then join the rows together.

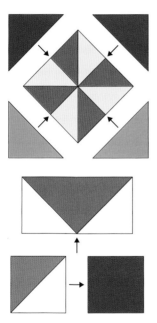

96 FIREBASKET AND CHAIN

A traditional basket block is filled with rather unconventional hot coals and separated by chain blocks for a quilt that really seems to glow. The key to achieving light in a quilt is to include a range of shades and tones, so that the lights can sparkle against the darks.

SUGGESTED LAYOUT

This design consists of two blocks, A and B. For my virtual quilt I have set nine of the Firebasket blocks (block A) and four of the Fire Chain blocks (block B) on point, separated by 1½" (3.8cm) finished sashing in an orange/red batik and 1½" (3.8cm) finished cornerstones in yellow. The large setting triangles are made from two squares cut at 15½" (39.4cm), cut on both diagonals to yield four setting triangles, and the corner triangles are cut from two squares at 8⅛" (20.6cm), cut on one diagonal to yield two triangles. Borders 1 and 3 finish at 1" (2.5cm). Border 2 finishes at 4" (10.2cm) bringing the quilt up to 61¼" x 61¼" (155.6 x 155.6cm).

For two Firebasket blocks you will need

Finished block size: 10" (25.4cm) square

- Four scraps of assorted red prints
- Three scraps of assorted orange prints
- Two scraps of assorted orange yellow prints
- One scrap of yellow print
- Three scraps of assorted brown prints
- Assorted cream and tan prints for the background

Assembling the Firebasket block

1. From the red, orange, orange/yellow and yellow prints cut a total of ten 2⅞" (7.3cm) squares, then cut them on one diagonal to yield twenty triangles. Keep one half for a second block – you will only need ten triangles.

2. From the assorted brown prints cut one 7⅞" (20cm) square and two 2⅞" (7.3cm) squares. Cut them on one diagonal to yield six triangles. Keep one large and two small triangles for your second block.

3. From the assorted cream/tan prints cut thirteen squares at 2⅞" (7.3cm). Cut them on one diagonal to yield twenty-six triangles (half for now and half for a second block). Cut one square at 4⅞"(12.4cm) and cut it on one diagonal to yield two triangles. Finally cut four rectangles, each 2½" x 6½" (6.4 x 16.5cm) – two for this block and two for your second block.

4. Make half square triangle (HST) units with all of the yellow, yellow/orange, orange and red prints and ten of the cream/tan triangles.

5. Join the HST units into rows as shown and add the remaining three cream/tan triangles to the right-hand edges of rows 2, 3 and 4. Join the rows.

6. Sew the large brown triangle to the bottom of the HST unit and press the seam towards the large triangle.

7. Sew one of the small brown triangles to the lower edge of a cream rectangle. Make two, noting the angle of the triangle is going the opposite way.

8. Join the rectangle/triangle units made in step 7 to the sides of the firebasket.

9. Sew the large cream triangle to the bottom corner of the block.

For one Fire Chain block you will need

Finished block size: 10" (25.4cm) square

- Nine assorted red/red orange 2½" (6.4cm) squares
- Four assorted cream/tan 2½" (6.4cm) squares
- Four assorted cream/tan 2½" x 6½" (6.4 x 16.5cm) rectangles

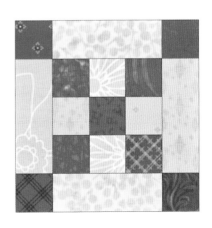

Assembling the Fire Chain block

1. Sew five of the red/orange squares and four of the assorted cream squares together into a nine-patch unit.

2. Sew a cream/tan rectangle to two opposite sides of the nine patch.

3. Sew a red/orange square to each end of the remaining cream/tan rectangles.

4. Sew the rectangle/square units to the last two sides of the nine patch.

97 ICE CRYSTALS

I love quilts with chain blocks in them – it's a great way to separate your pieced blocks and give them room to breathe. Here I've used one unifying background fabric, but you could use a variety of white on white scraps if you prefer.

SUGGESTED LAYOUT

For my virtual quilt I have set twelve Ice Crystal blocks (block A) together with thirteen Chain blocks (block B). The Chain blocks (see opposite) are made from the same four-patch units as in the Ice Crystal block, made with medium purple and white squares. You will need eight of these four-patch units per chain block. You will also need one dark purple 2½" (6.4cm) square for the centre, four 2½" (6.4cm) squares of white solid and four 2½" x 6½" (6.4 x 16.5cm) white rectangles. The outside border is made of Partial Chain blocks (block C) (see opposite), using five 1½" (3.8cm) squares of medium purple and 1½" (3.8cm) strips of white cut as follows: two 1½" (3.8cm), two 2½" (6.4cm), two 3½" (8.9cm) and two 4½" (11.4cm). The Partial Chain block finishes at 5" (12.7cm) square. You will need a total of 44 Partial Chain blocks to go around this quilt. The finished quilt is 60" x 60" (152.4 x 152.4cm).

For one Ice Crystals block you will need

Finished block size: 10" (25.4cm) square

- Sixteen dark turquoise 1½" (3.8cm) squares
- Four medium turquoise 2½" (6.4cm) squares
- Four medium turquoise 2⅞" squares, cut on one diagonal to yield eight triangles
- Sixteen white solid 1½" (3.8cm) squares
- Four white solid 2⅞" (7.3cm) squares, cut on one diagonal to yield eight triangles
- Eight dark purple 1½" (3.8cm) squares
- Four dark purple rectangles, each 1½" x 2½" (3.8 x 6.4cm)
- Four light green rectangles, each 1½" x 2½" (3.8 x 6.4cm)
- One medium purple 2½" (6.4cm) square

Assembling the Ice Crystals block

1. Pair up a white and a medium turquoise triangle, right sides together and sew together to make a half square triangle unit (HST) – see page 19. Make a total of eight HST units.
2. Sew two dark turquoise and two dark purple squares together, alternating the colours, to make a four patch. Make four of these units.
3. Sew two dark turquoise and two white squares together, alternating the colours, to make a four patch. Make four of these units.
4. Sew one light green and one dark purple rectangle together. Make four of these units.
5. Arrange the four-patch, HSTs, squares and rectangle units together around the central medium purple square. Sew the units into rows.
6. Sew the rows together.

Partial Chain block
(block C)

Chain block
(block B)

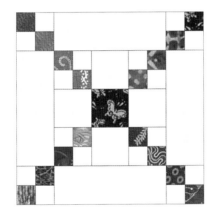

Ice Crystals block
(block A)

Try reversing the values, substituting a very dark background in place of the white and light medium tones in place of the turquoise and purple for a totally different look!

LITTLE HOUSES

I love these little red houses and I have updated the pattern to make it 'paper piecing friendly'. Don't be alarmed at the thought of joining multiple foundations together. Follow my tips for foolproof matching!

For one block you will need
Finished block size: 9" (22.9cm) square
- Scraps of red print for the house
- Scraps of cream print for the background

Assembling the block
1. Download and print (see page 224 for link) or photocopy one each of Little Houses foundations A,B,C and D (see page 238).
2. Following the general instructions for paper foundation piecing (page 21), piece the units in numerical order, trimming the seam allowances as you go.
3. Press and trim each unit to the seam allowance line.
4. Join A to B and C to D, then join the AB and CD units together.
5. Press the finished block carefully. Leave paper the intact until all the blocks have been sewn together.

When joining foundation-pieced units, sew the units together with a basting stitch, setting your sewing machine to sew the longest stitch length you can. Check that everything is matched well; if you're happy you can sew again using a shorter stitch.

SUGGESTED LAYOUT

For my virtual quilt I have set sixteen blocks together in four
rows of four and added five borders. Borders 1, 3 and 5
in gold finish at 1" (2.5cm), border 2 finishes at 3" (7.6cm).
Border 4 is pieced and is made of forty-four four-patch units,
each made up of two red, one cream and one tan 3" (7.6cm)
squares, so each four-patch unit finishes at 5" (12.7cm). You
will need eighty-eight red, forty-four cream and forty-four tan
squares. The quilt finishes at 58" x 58" (147.3 x 147.3cm).

PHARAOH'S TILES

Sometimes a scrap is a fat quarter or a bundle of half yard pieces you've fallen in love with but are afraid to cut into. Not a problem! Use this quilt pattern to showcase the prints by surrounding them with a garden maze sashing.

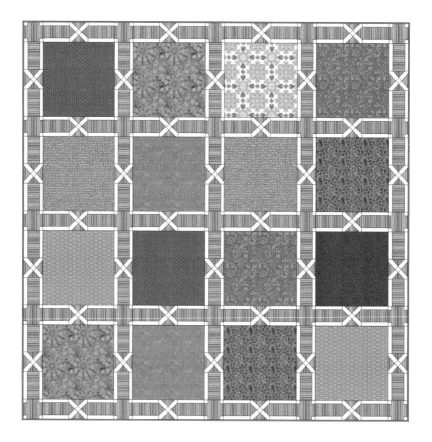

SUGGESTED LAYOUT

There isn't a 'block' as such, so I have provided the pattern for the whole quilt top. I added a binding of orange solid. The quilt finishes at 80" x 80" (203.2 x 203.2cm).

You will need

- 20" (½ metre) of eight feature prints or fat quarters of sixteen feature prints
- 2¾ yards (2½ metres) green and aqua print
- 2¼ yards (2 metres) solid cream

Assembling the quilt top

1. From each of the eight feature fabrics, cut two 15½" (39.4cm) squares (sixteen squares in total).

2. From the green and aqua print fabric, cut six strips 3" (7.6cm) wide x width of fabric (WOF) – 42" (106.7cm) – for sashing 1. From the same fabric, cut a further seven strips 3" (7.6cm) wide x WOF for sashing 2.

3. From the solid cream, cut twelve strips 1¼" (3.2cm) x WOF for sashing 1 and a further fourteen strips 1¼" (3.2cm) wide x WOF for sashing 2.

4. Make sashing 1. Join one solid cream 1¼" (3.2cm) strip to one 3" (7.6cm) green and aqua print strip. Press the seam allowances towards the cream fabric. Repeat with another solid cream strip on the opposite side of the same green and aqua print strip to make a strip-pieced unit that measures 4½" (11.4cm) wide x WOF. Make a total of six of these strip pieced units. Sub-cut into forty 6" x 4½" (15.2 x 11.4cm) segments. Set aside.

5. Make sashing 2 in exactly the same way, except that this time you will make seven strip-pieced units and then sub-cut into forty 6¾" x 4½" (17.1 x 11.4cm) segments.

6. Make the kiss block. From green and aqua print cut forty 4" (10.2cm) squares. Mark one diagonal lightly in pencil on the wrong side of each square.

7. From solid cream cut fourteen strips, each 1½" (3.8cm) x WOF. Sub-cut these into eighty 7" (17.8cm) long strips.

8. Take one of the 4" (10.2cm) green and aqua print squares cut in step 6. Do not cut on the pencil line: cut on the other diagonal and separate the two triangles. Sew one solid cream 1½" x 7" (3.8 x 17.8cm) strip in between the two triangles. There should be about 1" (2.5cm) of overhang at each end. Ensure that the pencil lines marking the diagonal run in a straight line.

9. Cut the square apart again, this time on the marked diagonal. Join another 1½" x 7" (3.8 x 17.8cm) solid cream strip in between the two triangles. Make sure the diagonals join up. Press the kiss unit, then trim the block to 4½" (11.4cm) square. Make sure that the 'kiss' runs through the centre of the ruler. Make a total of forty 'kiss' blocks.

10. Join one 6" (15.2cm) sashing 1 unit to each side of a kiss block. Make a total of twenty. Press the seam allowances one way.

11. Join one 6¾" (17.1cm) sashing 2 unit to each side of a kiss block. Make a total of twenty. Press the seam allowances one way.

12. From green and aqua print cut twenty-one rectangles, each 3" x 4½" (7.6 x 11.4cm).

13. From solid cream cut two strips, each 1¼" (3.2cm) x WOF. From these strips cut six rectangles, each 1¼" x 4½" (3.2 x 11.4cm). Add one of these rectangles to one side of six of the green and aqua print rectangles to make a 'rectangle + 1' unit.

14. Make sashing 2 as follows: rectangle +1, sashing 2, rectangle, sashing 2, rectangle, sashing 2, rectangle, sashing 2, rectangle +1. Make three of these strips.

15. From green and aqua print cut four rectangles, each 3" x 3¾" (7.6 x 9.5cm). From the remaining solid cream 1¼" (3.2cm) strips, cut four 3¾" (9.5cm) strips and four 4½" (11.4cm) strips. Sew a 3¾" (9.5cm) strip to the bottom of each of the green and aqua print rectangles. Press the solid cream strip back. Now sew a 4½" (11.4cm) solid cream strip to the adjacent side of each green and aqua print rectangle. Your block will resemble a letter L. You need two L blocks and two reverse L blocks for the outer corners of the quilt.

16. Sew the top and bottom sashing 2 strips as follows: L block, sashing 2, rectangle, sashing 2, rectangle, sashing 2, rectangle, sashing 2, reverse L block. Make two.

17. Arrange the sixteen 15½" (39.4cm) feature blocks on the floor or a design wall in four rows. Separate each block with a piece of sashing 1. Sew the sashing 1 pieces to the 15½" (39.4cm) feature squares. Make four rows.

18. Separate the four rows with sashing 2 rows. Put the top and bottom sashing 2 strips in place. Sew the rows together.

19. Press the quilt top well. Layer with batting (wadding) and backing cut to 88" x 88" (223.5 x 223.5cm).

100 MODERN CROSSES

A simple modern block, which will make great use of your modern scraps and black-and-white prints.

SUGGESTED LAYOUT

For my virtual quilt I have set sixteen Modern Crosses blocks in four rows of four with 1" (2.5cm) finished sashing and cornerstones in assorted black-and-white prints. The quilt finishes at 27" x 27" (68.9 x 68.9cm).

If you are using pre-cuts such as jelly roll strips, charm or layer cake squares for your quilting, you may prefer not to pre-wash the fabric. There will be a small amount of shrinkage when you pre-wash and your pre-cut won't be the right size any more!

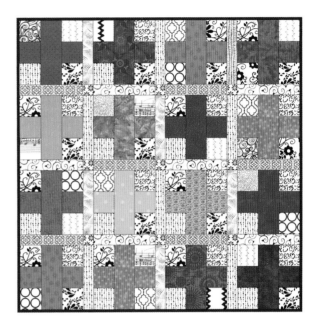

For one block you will need

Finished block size: 6" (15.2cm) square

- Four 2½" (6.4cm) squares of assorted black-and-white prints
- One assorted bright scrap cut into two 2½" (6.4cm) squares and one 2½" x 6½" (6.4 x 16.5cm) rectangle

Assembling the block

1. Sew a black-and-white print squares to opposite sides of a bright print 2½" (6.4cm) square. Make two units.
2. Join the units made in step 1 to each side of the 2½" x 6½" (6.4 x 16.5cm) bright scrap rectangle.

TEMPLATES

Photocopy the templates you need, at the size indicated, or go to www.pavilionbooks.com/make100quilts to download and print full-size templates. Make a test block before embarking on a whole quilt – measure the test block to make sure it has the correct dimensions as indicated in the instructions.

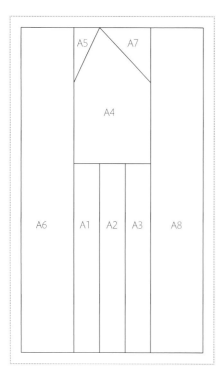

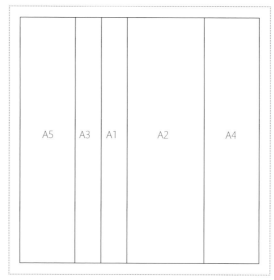

9 Lipstick and Polish foundations A–D Enlarge by 200%

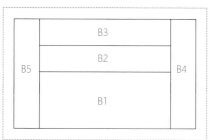

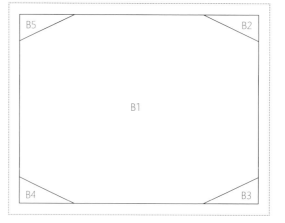

8 Stripping foundations A–D
Enlarge by 200%

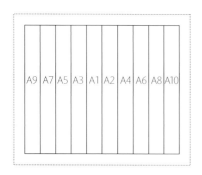

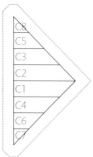

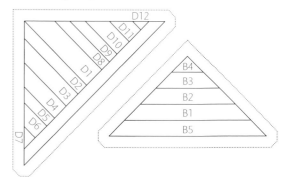

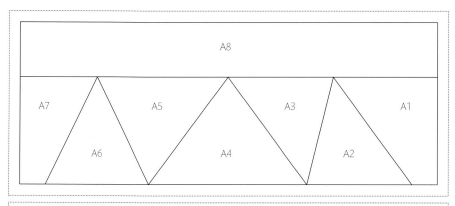

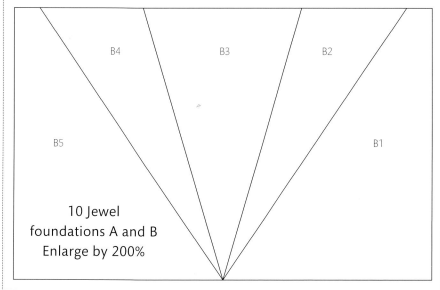

10 Jewel
foundations A and B
Enlarge by 200%

18 Zigzag
foundation A
Enlarge by 200%

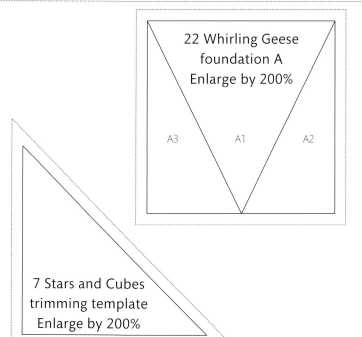

22 Whirling Geese
foundation A
Enlarge by 200%

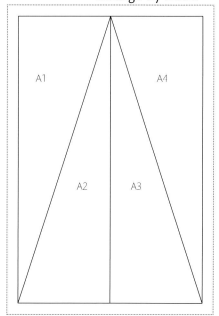

7 Stars and Cubes
trimming template
Enlarge by 200%

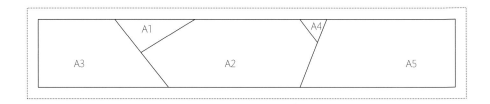

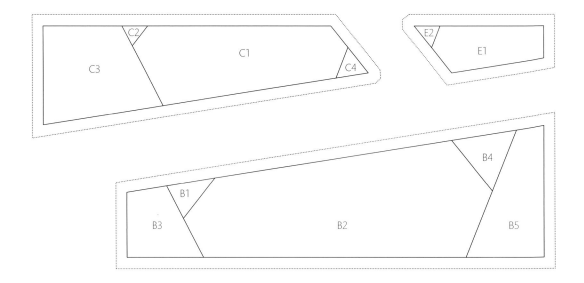

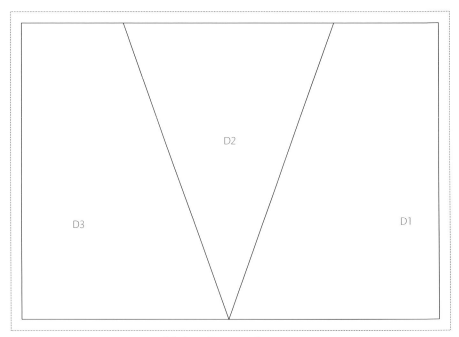

11 Ice Cream Cone
foundations A–D
Enlarge by 200%

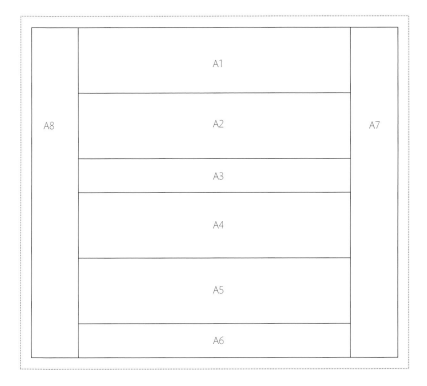

19 Spool of Thread
foundations A–C
Enlarge by 200%

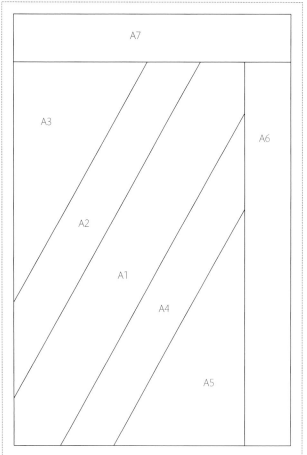

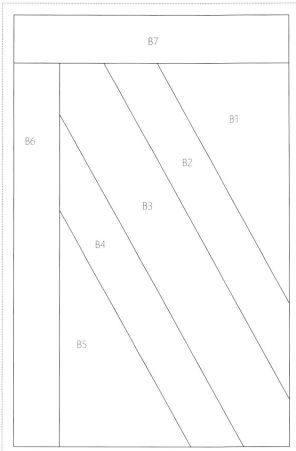

21 Union Jack
foundations A and B
Enlarge by 200%

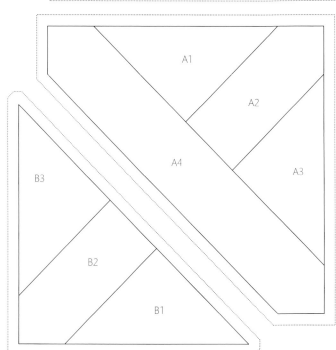

24 Latticework
foundations A and B
Enlarge by 200%

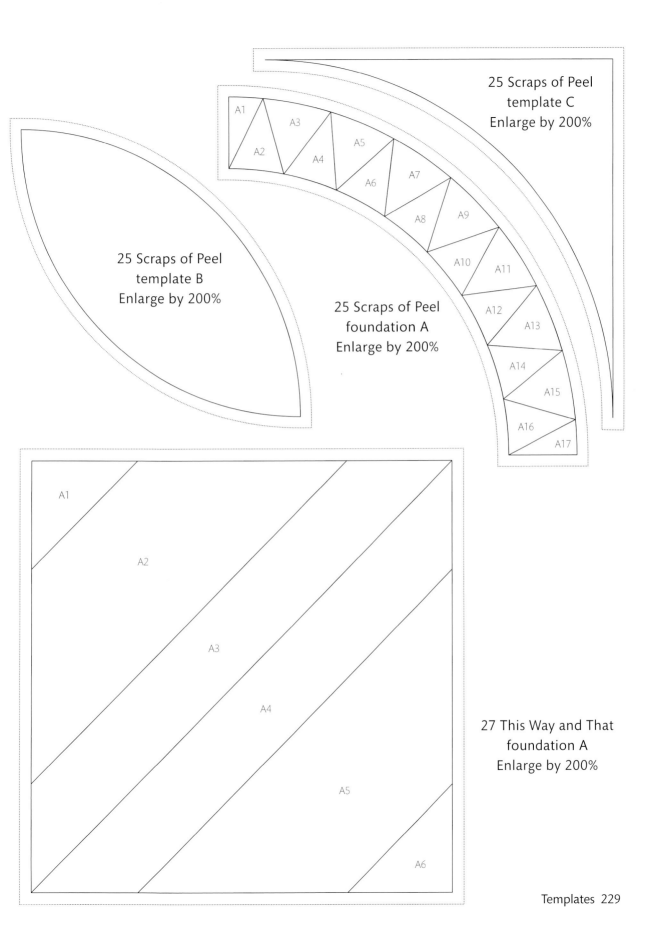

25 Scraps of Peel
template C
Enlarge by 200%

25 Scraps of Peel
template B
Enlarge by 200%

25 Scraps of Peel
foundation A
Enlarge by 200%

27 This Way and That
foundation A
Enlarge by 200%

Templates 229

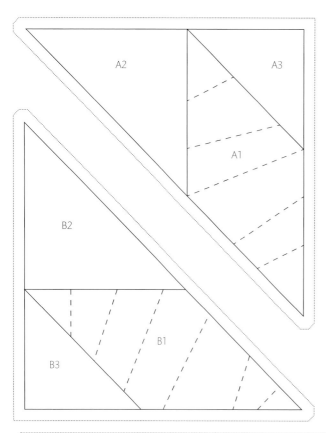

29 String Star
foundations A and B
Enlarge by 200%

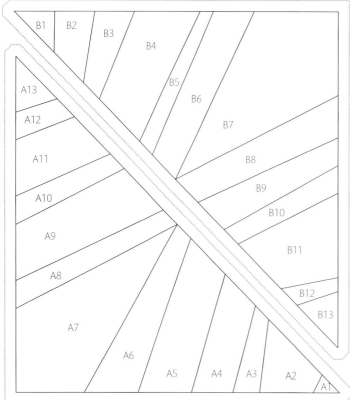

30 Spider's Web
foundations A and B
Enlarge by 200%

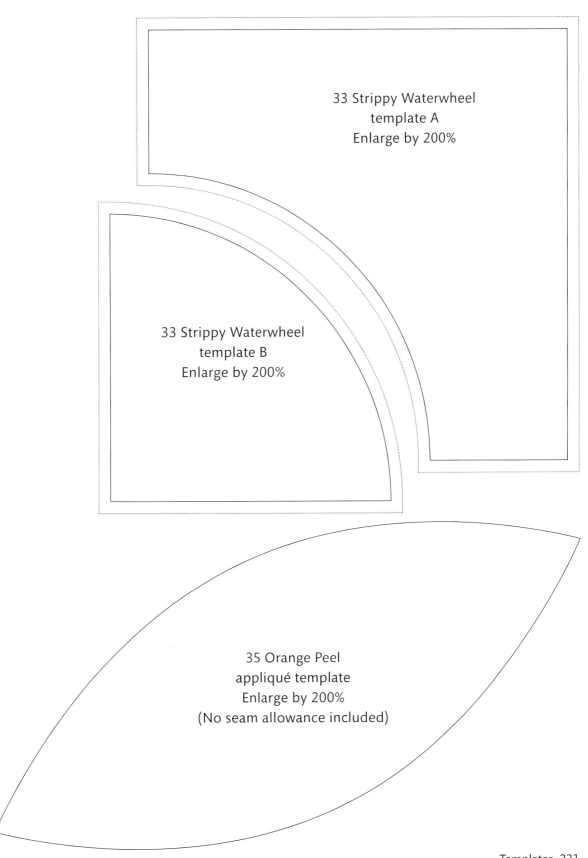

33 Strippy Waterwheel
template A
Enlarge by 200%

33 Strippy Waterwheel
template B
Enlarge by 200%

35 Orange Peel
appliqué template
Enlarge by 200%
(No seam allowance included)

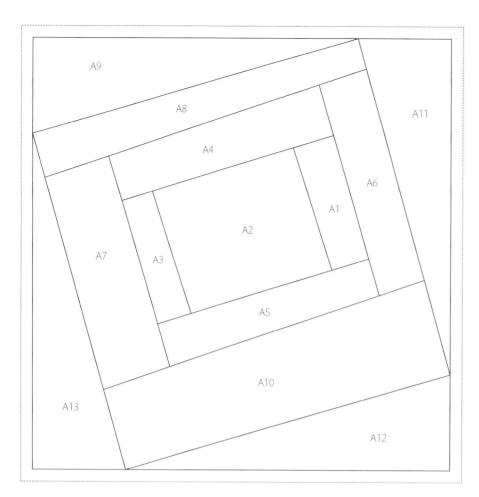

37 Wonky Boxes
foundation A
Enlarge by 200%

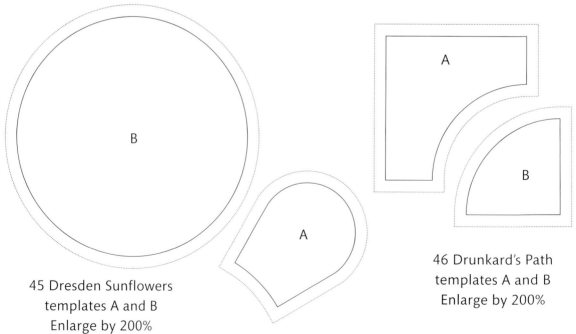

45 Dresden Sunflowers
templates A and B
Enlarge by 200%

46 Drunkard's Path
templates A and B
Enlarge by 200%

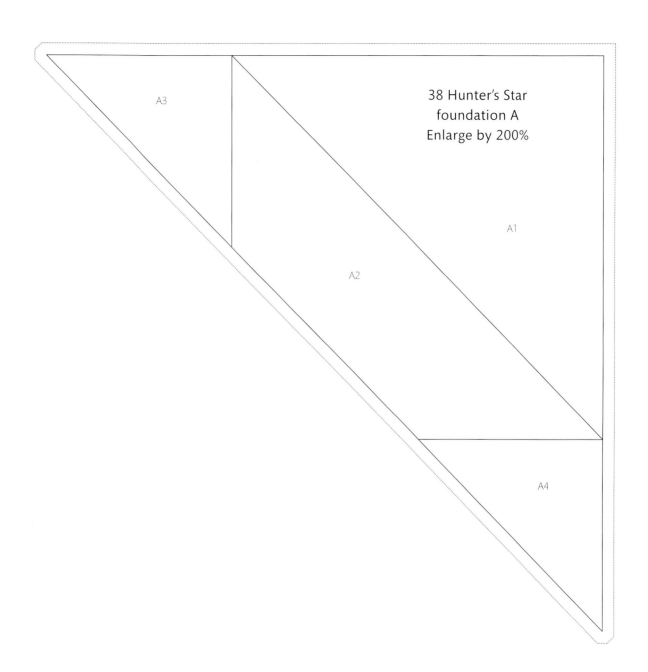

38 Hunter's Star
foundation A
Enlarge by 200%

A3

A1

A2

A4

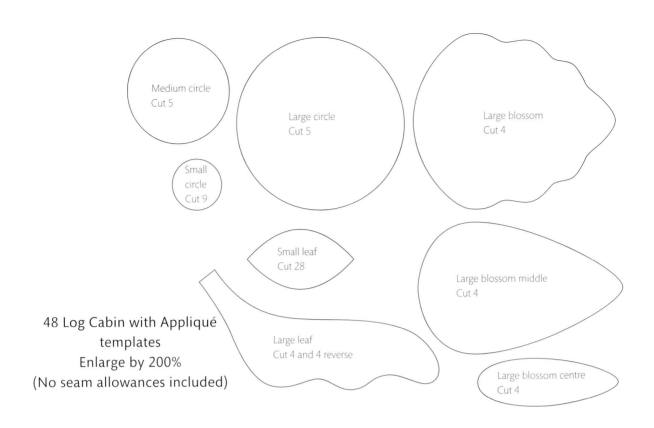

Medium circle
Cut 5

Small circle
Cut 9

Large circle
Cut 5

Large blossom
Cut 4

Small leaf
Cut 28

Large blossom middle
Cut 4

48 Log Cabin with Appliqué templates
Enlarge by 200%
(No seam allowances included)

Large leaf
Cut 4 and 4 reverse

Large blossom centre
Cut 4

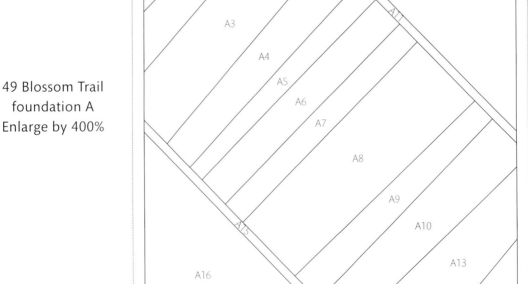

49 Blossom Trail
foundation A
Enlarge by 400%

A1
A2
A3
A4
A5
A6
A7
A8
A9
A10
A11
A12
A13
A14
A15
A16

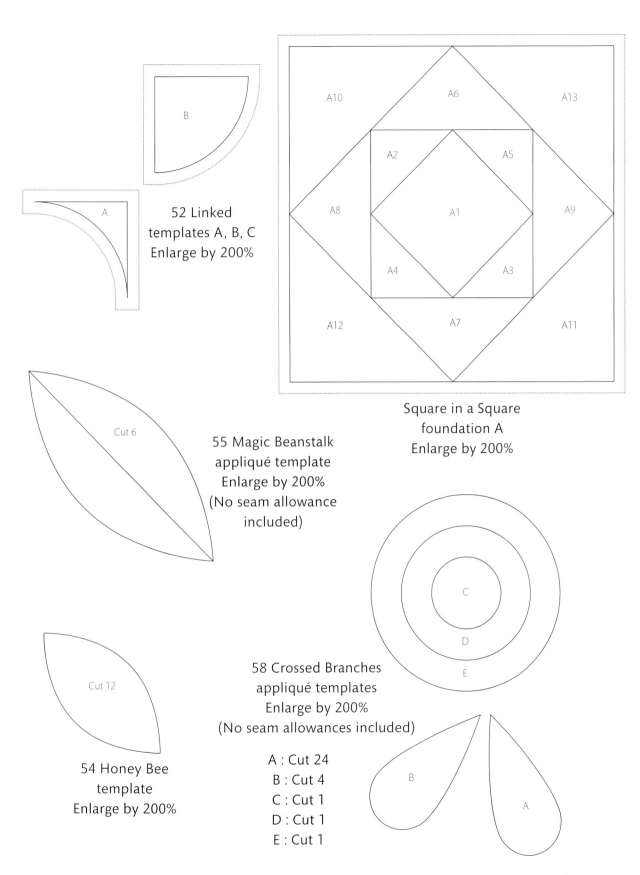

52 Linked
templates A, B, C
Enlarge by 200%

A10 A6 A13
A2 A5
A8 A1 A9
A4 A3
A12 A7 A11

Square in a Square
foundation A
Enlarge by 200%

Cut 6

55 Magic Beanstalk
appliqué template
Enlarge by 200%
(No seam allowance
included)

C
D
E

58 Crossed Branches
appliqué templates
Enlarge by 200%
(No seam allowances included)

Cut 12

54 Honey Bee
template
Enlarge by 200%

A : Cut 24
B : Cut 4
C : Cut 1
D : Cut 1
E : Cut 1

B
A

59 New York in the Spring
Block A
foundation A, D and E
Enlarge by 400%

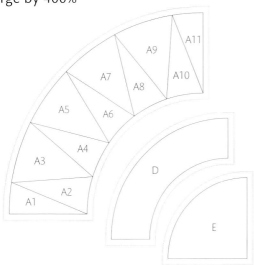

59 New York in the Spring
Block B
template C
Enlarge by 400%

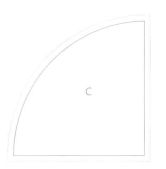

59 New York in the Spring
Block B
foundation A and B
Enlarge by 400%

59 New York in the Spring
Block A
templates B and C
Enlarge by 400%

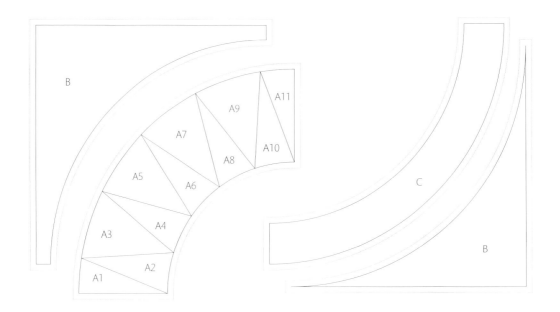

64 Mexican Fiesta
foundation A
Enlarge by 200%

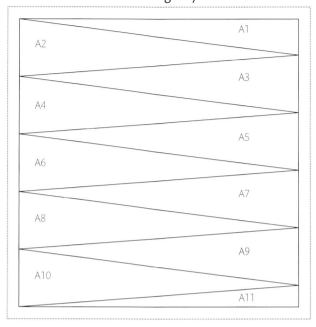

81 Scrappy Hearts
foundation A
Enlarge by 200%

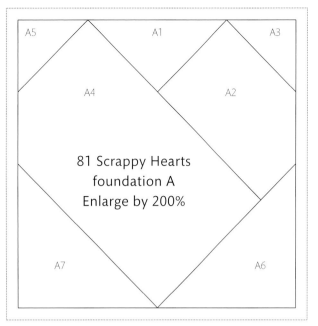

90 Peony
appliqué template
Enlarge by 200%

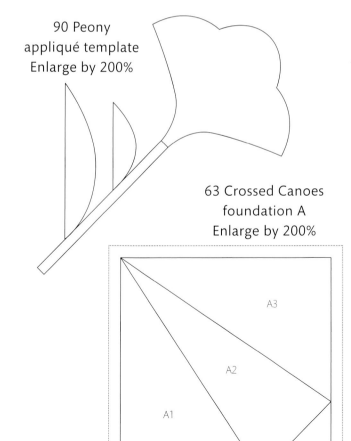

63 Crossed Canoes
foundation A
Enlarge by 200%

83 Geese Meet
foundation A
Enlarge by 200%

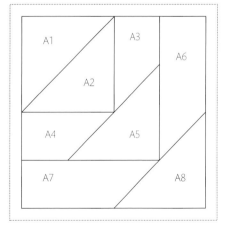

77 Star-spangled Banner
appliqué template
Enlarge by 200%
(No seam allowance included)

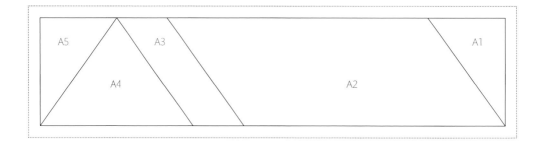

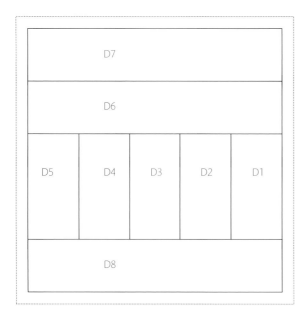

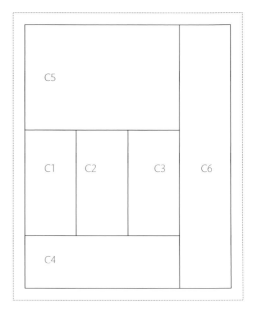

98 Little Houses
foundations A–D
Enlarge by 200%

SUPPLIERS

Sewing machines
Bernina
www.bernina.com

Quilting machines
Handi Quilter
For longarm quilting machines
www.handiquilter.com

Longarm quilting services
Mandy Parkes
www.quiltswhiskers.co.uk

Die cutting supplies
For Go! Cutting machines, strip dies, piecing and
appliqué dies
AccuQuilt
www.accuquilt.com

Machine sewing needles
www.schmetzneedles.com

Haberdashery
John Lewis
For general haberdashery, thread, template plastic, scissors
and rotary cutting equipment
www.johnlewis.com

Dunelm
For quilt batting (wadding), threads, general supplies
www.dunelm.com

Coats Thread
www.coats.com

Groves
For general haberdashery, 505 quilt basting spray, cotton
quilt battings (waddings), fusible web, Sew Easy rulers and
general cutting equipment
www.grovesltd.co.uk

Vliesofix
For fusible web, interfacings and battings (waddings)
www.vlieseline.com

Visage Textiles
For general haberdashery, cotton quilt battings (waddings)
www.visagetextiles.com

Barnyarns
For general haberdashery and quilting supplies
www.barnyarns.co.uk

Fabrics
Patchwork and quilting supplies, cutting equipment,
longarm quilting machines and supplies

The Cotton Patch
www.cottonpatch.co.uk

Lady Sew and Sew Fabrics
www.ladysewandsew.co.uk

Makower UK
www.makoweruk.com

The Craft Cotton Company
www.craftcotton.com

The Cosy Cabin
For general quilting supplies and quilting fabrics
www.thecosycabin.co.uk

Colouricious
Fabric printing supplies
www.colouricious.com

ACKNOWLEDGEMENTS

Just like a patchwork quilt, this book is a collection of many elements, gathered together to make something beautiful. I want to say heartfelt thanks to everyone who has been involved in this project and for your hard work, dedication, creativity and support.

To Heather, my wonderful agent, and to all at HHB who continue to guide, support and believe in me. To Katie, Amy and all at Pavilion who have helped me create a book that I am so proud of, I am truly grateful. Huge thanks also to Krissy, Michelle, Sophie, Rachel and Corin for making this book look so inviting and inspiring.

Very special thanks go to Joan Drake and Mandy Parkes, who helped me to make some of the quilts in this book. Your sewing skills are matched by your kindness, your talents and your friendship. I am truly blessed to have you in my life.

Finally to Charlie, my husband, whose support and belief in me is unwavering, whose ability to layer a quilt at 11pm is without equal and who helped me take the scraps, see their value and make a beautiful quilt together.

DEDICATION

This book is dedicated to every quilter who ever looked at their fabric stash and saw the glint of a quilt yet to be made. You are my quilting brothers and sisters and I wrote this book for you.

Photography by Rachel Whiting

First published in the United Kingdom in 2017 by
Pavilion
43 Great Ormond Street
London
WC1N 3HZ

ISBN 978-1-910904-56-5

A CIP catalogue record for this book is available from the British Library.

10 9 8 7 6 5 4 3 2

Reproduction by Mission, Hong Kong
Printed and bound by Imak Offset, Turkey

This book can be ordered direct from the publisher at www.pavilionbooks.com